LEAD OR BE LED 2.0

The Guide to A.C.E. Training

A CANINE EXPERIENCE INC.
SNOHOMISH WA

Written for *A Canine Experience, Inc.*

By Trina R Eddy

With contributions from:

Nancy Baer
Autumn Baer
Andrea Kelley

Book edited by:
Arlene Hulten
(Scout's Mom)

Cover photo taken by:
Autumn Baer

Cover photo edited by:
Stephanie Lester

TABLE OF CONTENTS

TABLE OF CONTENTS

TABLE OF CONTENTS

TABLE OF CONTENTS

TABLE OF CONTENTS

Acknowledgement

We, Andrea, Autumn and I, would like to give special thanks to both our parents for the knowledge and support they've given us.

Mom, Nancy Baer, began *A Canine Experience, Inc.* as a dog trainer's school in 1995, educating many current dog trainers who continue their practices, including ourselves. Upon her retirement, she offered us the opportunity to take over the 32-kennel, boarding and training business it had grown into. Without her shared knowledge, initiative, foresight and continued support, we would not be running the successful business we operate today.

Dad, Ralph Baer, despite his minimal interest in dogs has supported us in numerous ways. He has spent endless hours performing maintenance and repairs, building kennels, constructing doors and gates, rewiring buildings and adding lighting, educating us, making accommodations in difficult times and so much more I cannot begin to list.

The journey has not always been easy, but we have the good fortune of being born to amazing, supportive parents who provided us a good education with many opportunities, taught us to work hard, take responsibility, raised us with values, and always believe in us.

Preface

A Canine Experience, Inc. distributes *Lead or Be Led 2.0* in correlation with A.C.E. training programs and is dedicated to our valued customers who trust and support us with their beloved pets.

A Canine Experience, Inc. was founded by Nancy Baer in 1995 and is a multi-generational family establishment.

A Canine Experience, Inc. training programs are currently offered by Trina Eddy, Andrea Kelley and Autumn Baer. We believe in offering individualized services specific to the needs of our clients by incorporating a variety of methods and styles. Continuing education is a valued priority, implementing the most current research and techniques into our repertoire.

We aim to use a holistic approach to dog training, therefore gather information about the history, genetics, training, experiences, health, medications, diet, motivation, owner's goals and behavior of the dog. We use this information to determine the best training techniques and program for the situation.

Dog training is an ongoing process requiring commitment and consistency. Below is a copy of the Training Agreement used when booking a dog for ACE training programs.

A Canine Experience, Inc. Training Agreement

Overview of Programs

We offer specialized training programs, which begin with a thorough evaluation of your dog's behavior. We carefully design a plan best suited to you and your dog's needs. Our broad experience includes basic obedience, house manners, fearfulness, various aggression issues, specialty training in agility, scent work, fitness, engagement, genetics, breeder research, temperament testing, relationship building, games and much more.

If you choose to leave your dog(s) for training, he will learn basic obedience commands and improved self-control. Our goal is to make your dog the best he can be. We will coach you on continuing the training and managing his behavior. Every dog is on his own training schedule according to what is determined during the evaluation.

Two+ week Board & Train(B&T) and Lodging with Education(LW/E) Programs include the book *Lead or Be Led 2.0*, two private lessons, and one month of group class membership to immediately proceed the follow up lesson (*see note under recommendations). A Private Lesson will be scheduled for pick up and a follow-up lesson within the following two weeks.

Additional training programs include: Day Training, Private Lessons, Group

INTRODUCTION

Class Memberships, Specialized Classes and Workshops, Diabetic Alert Dog Co-Training and Service Dog Co-Training.

Trainers

Primary trainers are Andrea Kelley, Autumn Baer and Trina Eddy. If you have any questions or concerns, please discuss them with a trainer only.

Training Methods

We incorporate positive based training techniques. Equipment and methods will vary depending on the dog's prior training, current behaviors, willingness, drive and needs.

Limitations

Each dog is a unique individual and results will vary. The amount of work and follow through by the owner will have a huge impact on the success of training. Dog training is an ongoing process and will only be successful if owners follow through with consistent leadership and structure.

Expectations

We only bring dogs in for training if the owners are committed to the training program and agree to follow through as instructed.
If you are having unsolvable challenges after taking your dog home from training, call immediately and speak to a trainer for help. DO NOT wait until the problem develops further to call. Immediate attention is needed if your dog is not performing as discussed and demonstrated.
Please DO NOT ask non-trainer employees for training advice or press them to answer questions.

Disclosure

Training results will vary depending on the individual dog's temperament, previous experiences, behavior and the owner's follow through.
Obedience is a diminishing skill that will decline quickly without practice and persistence.

INTRODUCTION

Requirements

All Training Programs
Complete an Evaluation Questionnaire.
Bring Questionnaire and your dog(s) to a scheduled in-person Behavioral Evaluation.
Read the book *Lead or Be Led 2.0*.
Follow the procedures defined in the *Lead or Be Led 2.0* book.
Implement a variety of exercises from the *Lead or Be Led 2.0* book.
Practice exercises in a variety of environments.
Follow the individualized instructions provided by your trainer.

Board & Train and Lodging w/ Education
Participate in a Private Go Home lesson when picking up from B&T and Lw/E Programs.
Participate in a Follow-up lesson one-two weeks after going home from B&T or Lw/E Programs.

Day Training
Commit to three-four training days per week for the first three-four weeks.
Participate in a Private Lesson after two weeks.
Participate in a Private Lesson at three-four weeks.
Participate in a minimum of one monthly Private Lesson with ongoing training.

Group Class Memberships
Participate in minimum of two Private Lessons prior to beginning Group Class.
Participate in additional Private Lessons if needed.
Approval to attend Group Classes is required.
Attend Group Classes regularly once approved.

Recommended
All family members over 10 years of age participate in lessons and classes.
Attend group classes during the month following completion of the Board & Train and Lodging w/ Education programs*.
Continue with Beyond Board and Train Group Class Membership.

INTRODUCTION

Participate in group classes in conjunction with Day Training.

> *Dogs with aggression issues are not allowed into group classes unless a reliable management plan has been developed. Group classes may not be optimal for extremely insecure or shy dogs. Your trainer will discuss appropriateness and options in these cases.

I have read and understand *A Canine Experience, Inc.'s* training programs requirements and agree to commit to the terms. This commitment comprises of the above listed requirements and will include additional instructions.

Signature   _____

Date   _____

Part 1- Communication with Your Canine

What is Leadership?

Leadership is the art of motivating a person, or in our context a dog, to act towards a common goal and developing them in a way to reach their full potential.

If you Google "Qualities of a Great Leader" you will consistently see lists including honesty, integrity, confidence, inspirational, motivating, committed, passionate, clear communicator, decisive, accountable, influential, optimistic, empowering, creative, empathetic and resilient. While these lists are geared towards people and organizations, the same principles apply when working with dogs.

In our case, great leaders are not heavy handed or gruff, rather they find ways to motivate their dog to want to achieve the desired goal. Leaders understand and use to their advantage one basic principle: *Reinforcement drives behavior.*

Training at Home

It is imperative that you continue your dog's education at home to ensure ongoing improvement.

It is important to be consistent about enforcing the new rules and start incorporating games and commands right away. As you leave ACE, have your dog "Wait" at the door and gate. Practice proper leash handling on your way to the car and reinforce your dog's engagement with you. Ask your dog to sit and wait while you open the car door and maintain the position until you release him to jump in.

When you arrive home, have your dog "Wait" to get out of the car. Practice proper leash handling going up to the house and have him "Wait" at the door before entering. Do a short training session once inside. Practice having your dog sit, down and going to his bed or platform. Have some fun by doing a few tricks or playing a constructive game. This helps your dog understand the things he has learned will now be expected at home. Incorporate what he's learned into your daily routines, develop new patterns and generalize hid training into new environments.

It is okay to pet and love your dog, but don't allow your dog to jump on you, put his mouth or feet on you, or get on the furniture without an invitation. It can be helpful to leave a leash on your dog when you are home so you can easily monitor his behavior without grabbing or chasing.

Take your time, be patient and work through the commands. Help your dog understand the new rules by being consistent and rewarding the behaviors you like.

You can feel confident your dog understands the commands we trained and demonstrated to you, but dogs do not generalize well. You and other members of the household must practice in a variety of environments. Start with areas with a low level of distraction and advance to busier areas as you and your dog excel.

Your dog will try to go back to previously known behaviors at home. Be prepared for your dog to test the boundaries. Persistence and follow through will pay big dividends during this phase. Stay attentive and set yourself up for success by crating, using back ties or placing in a secure area when distracted. Use your house lead to work through any issues until your dog responds, then positively reinforce the desired behavior.

Inexpensive, high value treats can be made by chopping and baking chicken or beef hotdogs. See instructions below.

Hotdog Baking Instructions:

1. Preheat oven to 400.
2. Cut hotdogs into 4 pieces the long way, then slice into ¼" – ½" pieces.
3. Spread out in a thick layer across a baking sheet.
4. Bake in oven about 45-minutes
5. Use a spatula to mix well every 10-15 minutes until done.
6. Cook until fairly browned throughout. I prefer a bit crispy.
7. Store in baggies or containers in the refrigerator or freezer.

PART 1 – COMMUNICATION WITH YOUR CANINE

TIP 1: Divide hotdogs into snack packs, place in a quart or gallon size freezer bag and store in the freezer. This makes it very convenient to grab one for day use. Store any leftovers in the refrigerator for future use.

TIP 2: We use chicken or beef hotdogs that come in the value pack. Avoid sausage, it is very greasy.

TIP 3: The jumbo-sized hotdogs can be sliced long ways into six or nine pieces, before being chopped.

Vocabulary

Break: This command marks a behavior and clearly lets your dog know he is done working. Release your dog from a behavior with a cheerful "Break" and reward with a treat, toy, or play. You can toss the treat or toy or have him come to you for the reward after you give the release. A good strategy is to toss the treat to a location that will set your dog up for another repetition.

There should be a pause between the word "Break" and the delivery of the reward. "Break" reinforces what they are doing the moment you say it, buying you time to deliver the reward. The rewarding event begins the moment you start reaching for the reward. Think of it as a four-step dance: say "Break", pause, reach for the reward, deliver the reward.

Come: This command is used to have your dog come directly to you and is strictly a positive command. Optimally we would like him to come, sit in front of us, give us eye contact and hold the position until released. He can be taught to come to a whistle, beep on a remote collar, or other sounds. See Coming Steps and Games in the Constructive Games & Exercises section for steps to a good come.

Here is a bit on coming from the *Puppy Culture* DVD series.
Come to Me- Recall
Most breeders use a puppy call when they put food down, a powerfully conditioned reinforcer. Puppies naturally move toward high pitch, fast sounds. Even if the breeder didn't use a puppy call, you can start by incorporating one when putting the food down.

You can then start adding a recall que to the puppy call to pair. The que will become equally exciting and you can gradually fade the puppy call.

Caveats- this works because you are creating a classically conditioned, involuntary feeling of excitement. To maintain this feeling, you MUST give something fantastic when they come to you. Praise may work when they are small, but by 16 weeks of age, food becomes most preferred form of currency.

Dogs hear in music or tones, so you must always call the same way. Use a tone you would not normally speak in and only means come to you. (Killion et.al.)

Correction: Corrections can be applied in a variety of ways. Basically, a correction is something that the dog does not enjoy. A quick pop with the leash, pressure from the leash, a firm "No," body pressure, a distracting sound or spray of water are forms of corrections sometimes used to stop an unwanted behavior.

Sensitive dogs may be corrected with just a verbal chastising such as a low tone "no" or "ah ah," a stern look, or overpowering posture.

For dogs who solicit or demand attention ignoring the dog and or stepping or turning away is also a form of correction.

Down: "Down" means lay down (not get off) and is used for various exercises and managing behavior. When working on down, leave the leash and collar attached and have your dog remain down until released. If your dog gets up before you say "Break," say "No," take hold of the leash, put him back where you originally had him and ask him to "Down" again.

If he understands the command and is unresponsive, you can give a downward leash correction or apply constant downward pressure until he complies. Have realistic expectations, try to set him up to be successful and build duration over time. If you are reinforcing frequently, he should be eager to comply.

Get It: Use "Get It" to let your dog know it's okay to go get a treat or toy. Rewards are used in a variety of ways. At times we use them to work on self-control, leave it or as a distraction. Other times, we incorporate games tossing treats that we want them to go after. Using "Get It" makes it clear to your dog when it is okay to go get the treat or toy.

Good: "Good" is a very important reinforcement word. "Good," in a happy voice, lets your dog know that he has done something right. We use "Good" as a hold word meaning, I like what you're doing, keep doing it.

Mark a desired behavior with "Good" the moment it is offered, then deliver a treat to the dog while he continues the behavior. There should be a pause between the word "Good" and the delivery of the treat. "Good" reinforces what they are doing the moment you say it, buying you time to give the reward.

You can increase duration by extending the time before releasing, but don't ask for too much too quickly. Try to release your dog before he breaks on his own. Slowly extending the duration, saying "Good" and rewarding him intermittently while he maintains the position or continues the behavior.

Implied Stay: It is implied when you ask your dog to get into a position or on a place, he remains until released or asked to do something else. If you ask your dog to "Down" or "Sit", he should remain in that position until you say "Break" or ask for another behavior. If asked only to "Place", the position is optional, but he should remain within the boundaries with all four feet.

I do not recommend asking your dog to hold a sit for longer than a minute or so unless they've been conditioned to do so. Down is a much more comfortable position for a dog to hold for an extended length of time.

Leash Pop: A pop on the leash given by you or as a side effect of your dog hitting the end of the leash. By conditioning your dog to move towards you when they feel the pressure, you can create a positive association with the pop. Do this by giving the leash a little pop, then luring him to you with a treat. Apply a light pop and hold out a treat for your dog to come and get. Repeat pop, reward, pop, reward until your dog begins returning to you when feeling the pop. You can use your movement and luring to help him move towards you. Do this several times until he automatically returns to you for a treat when feeling the pressure. Once he understands the feeling of the pressure means to return to you, add more movement. If he gets distracted or pulls ahead, turn away, pop the leash and reward when he returns. Once he understands, make a game of trying to catch him off guard. He'll be tough to lose.

Leave It: Use the "Leave It" command when your dog gets distracted by something. A good way to practice this command is by having your dog on a leash, dropping treats and having him "Leave It" by luring away with another treat, toy or encouragement. You can also place some enticing objects on the floor, walk past, say "Leave It," lure away several steps with a treat or toy, then reward. Be sure your dog is engaged with you and not still focused on the object he is leaving. If he understands "Leave It" and doesn't respond, give him a verbal "No" and/or leash pop and reward him when he turns away from the distraction. This command can be used for sniffing other animals, people, dropped food, etc.

Let's Go: This command lets your dog know that you want him to move with you. You can shorten the leash to keep him close or give more leash for a relaxed walk. Either way, we want the dog attentive to the handler, heeding to pressure.

Your leash can be short without being tight. If there is tension in the leash, we want the dog to learn to move or change pace to release the pressure. This can be taught by positively associating the pop of the leash to moving closer to you for a reward. (See Leash Pop.)

Use your movement to help your dog understand his responsibility. When he pulls ahead, make a quick 180° turn in the opposite direction. If he gets distracted and wanders away, exaggerate the mistake by moving in the opposite direction without lengthening the leash. If he's conditioned to a leash pop, apply as you turn away. Move with intent and expect him to follow. Reward when he moves back towards you.

Another strategy is to make every step count. If he pulls forward, stop until he releases the tension. Take a step and stop again if he forges or pulls. Wait until he releases the tension and repeat. This technique takes patience, you cannot have a distance goal. This is about patience and allowing the dog the opportunity to figure out they do not get to move forward when there is tension.

We want to encourage being attentive and checking in, so we want to reward eye contact and self-control. As you're walking watch for your dog to give you a glance. Each time he looks at you mark with "Good" and deliver a treat, while in motion. As he makes the connection that looking at you earns a reward, start holding out a little longer. Get two or three steps, then reward. Keep the number of steps between the rewards variable. Here's an example in number of steps with eye contact between rewards: 1,1,1,1,1,1,1,2,1,2,2,3,1,3,1,4,2,5,2,2,1,1, 5 jackpot reward and quit. This is just an example and may be too much for some dogs, especially at a beginning level.

Use a cycling down process in high distraction environments by maintaining a neutral demeanor while walking in large circles. Place your dog on the outside of the circle and walk at a consistent pace until he settles down. Some dogs settle down more easily walking quickly, others get more stimulated by the quick movement and do better at a slower pace. Watch for any engagement and reward.

If your dog is over stimulated with the environment, you will not be able to get him to focus. Walking calmly in big circles helps dog's cycle down in a stimulating environment. When he is ready to engage, he will start looking to you and behaving more calmly. This is your cue that he is ready to begin working. If he is not calming down, move to a less stimulating environment.

Manding: A good breeder will have already taught the concept of asking for things by sitting. Upon approaching the pen, ignore your puppy if he's jumping and only give attention or let out when he's sitting. Have every visitor follow the same approach. You may need to start by rewarding your puppy for four on the floor. Be patient and let your puppy figure out the behavior without you telling him. Once he's consistently sitting for people, work with a stationary dog and build up to a dog in motion. Get in the habit of waiting for your puppy to sit before you offer food or attention.

No: The word "No," stated firmly, makes it very clear to your dog that he is doing something wrong. Only use "No" when your dog is doing something he should not be doing, then reward with "Good" when he does what you ask. "Ah ah" or other low tones can be used in lieu of

"No," a bit less harsh for sensitive dogs.

"No" can be used to cut off an exercise when the dog has made a mistake. You can then reset him to the beginning of the exercise and give him the opportunity to perform correctly.

Off: Use this command to keep your dog's feet on the ground.
You may use the "Off" command to remind your dog not to jump up even before he attempts to jump. For example, if your dog usually jumps on you when you come home, say "Off," as soon as you open the door, instead of waiting until your dog jumps up. Follow the "Off" command by redirecting the jumping behavior to a sit. Ask for a "Sit" and do not give him any attention until he does. If he gets up when you reach down to pet him, pull your hands back, stand up straight and keep working on sit. Practice until you can pet him while he remains in the sit position. Be patient, it may take a bit of time for him to settle down and figure out the new routine.

Do not force him into a sit, allow him to think and learn from the process. He only gets attention when sitting, it goes away if he gets up. If he is overly exuberant, you can attach a house lead and put your foot on it so when he jumps up, he self-corrects. Stay calm, be patient, persistent and consistent.

Use this command to keep your dog from jumping up on people, furniture and counters. Attach a leash to the collar so you can guide or correct as needed. Only leave the leash attached to the collar when you are supervising.

Okay: Optional release command allowing you dog to come through a door or gate or to take a treat from your hand. Use a neutral voice to maintain a calmer demeanor.

Place: Used to have your dog go into or on any specific place. A place can be a pedestal, bench, pad, throw rug, log, block, box, hoop, wire spool, chair, etc. Sending your dog to a place when over stimulated is a practical way to redirect undesired behaviors.

Have your dog remain on the object until you release with "Break" or ask for something else. He can be in any position as long as he stays on the place. This allows him to move around and change positions.

You can ask for a position on an object. We then want him to hold that position until released or asked to do something else. If he starts to get off the object tell him, "NO, Place." If he succeeds at getting off the object before being released, calmly circle him around, re-approach the object and say "Place." Work on the duration before you add distance. Keep a hold on the leash, stay close and add movement working your way in a circle around your dog.

Once he is staying in place while you circle around him, extend the leash, step back increasing the distance, then work to walk around him from further away. Incrementally increase the distance as duration improves.

Make sure you're not asking too much of your dog. If the object is difficult and he is becoming fatigued, it is not fair to keep pushing him. Watch for signs of fatigue and allow periods of rest as needed to keep your dog safe and comfortable.

To increase the distance sending him to a place, teach him to go to a target (like a paper plate) for a treat or toy. Start close and increase the distance. Once he is familiar with going to a target, use the target on the object to send your dog to place. You may need to guide him onto the object to help him understand to get on it, otherwise, he may just go eat the treat. Start close and increase the distance as he becomes reliable at getting on it. Once he understands the objective, you can send him to place without a target, mark with "Good" when he gets on it, then reward. He should be comfortable getting on the object before you try these steps.

Be reasonable, keep expectations realistic and know the ability level of your dog. Pay attention to what he is telling you. If he is resistant, recognize if the object is too difficult, or if he is tired or sore.

If it's a simple, familiar object and he is too distracted to get on it, you can get his attention by luring and/or guide him with the leash. Circling out and back to the object often helps to get them refocused.

If it's an unfamiliar or difficult object, you can try luring, allowing him to sniff, test with his front feet and see if he will attempt with all four. You can place a handful of food or a couple treats on an object, step back and allow your dog to check it out. DO NOT force him onto an obstacle. Refer to the section "Time to Think."

Remember to praise your dog with a happy "Good" and a pet or treat when he gets on the object and reward sporadically while remaining in place.

Out: "Out" is used to ask your dog to release a toy. We often train the out by using two toys or by tossing treats. By making the active toy go dead and the other come alive, we can develop a release without a struggle. Some dogs will release easily in exchange for a treat and we can create a positive association with giving up the toy. Avoid putting pressure on your dog to recover the toy, this will build conflict into your game.

Praise: Look for opportunities to reward your dog for behaving the way you like. Praise can be petting, verbal, treats, toys or playtime. The praise should match the task that has been accomplished. If your dog has just figured out a difficult training exercise, you may have a big party with treats falling from the sky and lots of enthusiasm. If your dog has completed a simple, known task like sit, you may just give a positive verbal reward. Don't be stingy with your rewards.
Remember: *Reinforcement Drives Behavior.*

Sit: Used for various exercises and managing behavior. We also work towards an auto-sit when stopping. If your dog understands the command and doesn't sit when asked, you may give an upward leash correction, say "No" and ask to sit again. You can also step into your dog, applying a little upward leash pressure to encourage him to sit.

He should remain in a sit until you release him with "Break" or ask him to do something else. Sitting is not comfortable for dogs to maintain for long periods of time, so keep expectations reasonable. Build duration slowly and watch for fatigue.

Stand: Stand is useful for many reasons such as grooming, tricks or canine fitness. This can be a challenging position for dogs to learn on cue. You can start with him in a sit or down. From a sit position you can use a treat at nose level and lure straight forward, mark with "Good" and reward once in a stand. If he is in a down, lure slightly up and forward. Teach the stand from both a sit and a down position.

Touch: This command is typically used to teach to your dog to touch his nose to a target. The target can be your hand, lid or target stick. Once taught, targeting can be used to lure or to redirect your dog. Start teaching by presenting the target, saying "Good" and rewarding for a nose touch. Most dogs are naturally curious and will investigate, capture the opportunity to mark and reward when he does. While he is eating the treat, move the target out of sight and re-present. If he doesn't touch the target on his own, mark and reward for looking at the target and any movement towards it. Be patient, break it down to simplify and reward frequently. Do not push the target towards him or put it in his face.

Wait: Use this command when going in and out of doors and cars. This is used for safety as well as establishing leadership. When you arrive home, make sure your dog waits before getting out of the car and before entering the house. You and the family should enter the house and he should offer you eye contact before you give the "Okay" command for your dog to enter the house. We want his focus on you before releasing. If your dog breaks and goes through the door before you say "Okay," take him back out and start over until he waits properly. Consistently use this command at all doors and gates.

Working for Meals

We highly recommend using your dog's meals as rewards during training sessions. Working for meals is natural for dogs and helps build their desire to engage with you. This is a great opportunity to build your relationship, solidify some basic commands and establish good eye contact.

A training session could be a series of sits, downs and stands incorporating eye contact. Give a handful of food at a time. If they have a breakthrough, you could jackpot the remainder of the meal.

Meals could be used to begin scent training, by dividing into portions and hiding under training aids or in bowls or boxes scattered about. They earn the food as they find it. If you are short on time, you could offer their meal in a treat stick, ball or snuffle pad designed to make them work for it. There are many options available and these are great to use in a crate. Be creative and mix it up day to day.

If your dog is not food motivated, this procedure can help. You can add canned food to make the meal more enticing. If your dog refuses to eat, put the meal away and try again later. Do not give other treats during this time. Most dogs will begin eating better after 2-3 days. This is important, especially if your dog is unmotivated by play or attention.

Many dogs who have never had to earn attention, food or playtime are resistant to training and we need to build in a motivator. To do this, these dogs need to learn to earn their food and attention by not getting them for free.

Understanding Eye Contact

There seems to be a lot of confusion about eye contact. Should you or should you not look a dog directly in the eyes? Or allow a dog to look directly into your eyes? There is no single answer to this question.

Eye to eye contact is very important for dog communication. How you look at a dog depends on what you are trying to communicate. If you are trying to convince a dog you are dominant and in charge, you may give him a stern glare. If you lock eyes with the dog, looking away is a sign of submission. Eye contact is not the only thing dogs consider, they also watch your facial expressions and body language.

When I am training my dogs, I encourage them to look at my eyes and I look directly into theirs. This does not mean they are challenging me; it means they are engaged in the training or activity. Eye contact is very desirable when working with a dog.

Many insecure dogs will not look you in the eye. Their training will include building their confidence up enough that they feel comfortable looking you in the eye. Do not intimidate these dogs with strong eye contact and body language because this will make them more insecure. Acclimation and engagement exercises will help to build their confidence.

I have trained dogs that refused to give me any eye contact. Sometimes they turn their body and face the other direction. This behavior is often indicative of a very insecure dog, but some are spoiled dogs who don't want to acknowledge me, a rebellious act.

Direct eye contact with a dog is sometimes a very relaxed, happy experience. A study from *Science* revealed an increase in oxytocin in both human and dog when gazing into each other's eyes when it is voluntary and unsolicited.

> If you think of your dog as your "fur baby," science has your back. New research shows that when our canine pals stare into our eyes, they activate the same hormonal response that bonds us to human infants. The study—the first to show this hormonal

bonding effect between humans and another species—may help explain how dogs became our companions thousands of years ago. (Grimm)

Time to Think

Have you ever been in a situation where you were learning something new, understood the process, but it wasn't committed to muscle memory, so you still had to think it through?

Have you had that same situation with someone lurking over your shoulder? Watching to see if you do it right?

How does that make you feel? Can you complete the task?

Could you complete the task if the person walked away and gave you a minute to think it through?

This happens to me frequently when using computers, an area in which I am challenged. We recently incorporated a new scheduling program, designed by an app company. I had to do a lot of work to customize it for our business. I thought being the one customizing the program would help me understand the operational side, so I jumped into the project knowing it would be a challenge.

About five months later, after much tweaking and testing, we went live. My brain was overloaded with mounds of new information, new processes, ongoing modifications, customer questions and issues, employee questions, complaints and requests.

I would have a customer or employee standing in front of me and I would struggle to recall even a simple process. Often co-workers would step in to help or do it for me. This frustrated me, because given a minute, I would figure it out. I wasn't going to learn if people kept doing it for me or directing me through it. I just needed a minute to think it through.

As I worked through the process more times, it became easier and more intuitive. If a new challenge arises, I can usually figure it out given a little time and maybe some direction. Generally, I just need a minute to think.

I'm sure you're asking what this has to do with dog training, I assure you it is very relevant.

PART 1 – COMMUNICATION WITH YOUR CANINE

During an initial evaluation with an owner and dog, we gather as much information about the dog's history, prior training, successes and challenges, the environment, owner's lifestyle, health etc. Often when we discuss previous training and methods, we find gaps in the process creating confusion or lack of trust. We often see dogs being forced into a position or physically restrained. The dogs are frequently overstimulated when first entering our facility making it difficult for them to listen. Many owners are unsure how to manage the dog, the dog doesn't understand the expectations and hasn't learned to have self-control. That is why they are here.

We work with the owners and dogs on their skills and establishing a mutually beneficial, respectful relationship. There are numerous methods to get a dog to respond, but generally you can lure them to help them understand the behavior you want, physically force them into a position, or condition them by marking and rewarding desired behaviors.

Luring can be helpful when trying to teach something new, especially a behavior that is not natural for your dog. You can use food, a toy or stick to have them follow- moving up, down, left, right, forward, back, over, under, on, and side to side to teach them movements while creating positive associations.

Luring should be diminished as the dog better understands the desired behavior. Luring is not an effective way to develop cognitive thinking skills. Continuing with this method too long results in lazy thinkers who are dependent on constant input. Our goal is to create a clear method of communication with your dog, so we need them to respond to our cues without guidance. It is common to have difficulties moving away from luring and developing a dog who responds quickly and willingly without assistance.

Physically forcing dogs doesn't promote learning and can diminish trust, often resulting in a less willing dog. Force includes pushing, pulling, lifting or restraining with a leash or anywhere on their body. Intimidation with your body, stern eye contact and/or voice is also forceful.

There are times when force or restraint are useful or necessary; however, force or restraint being used in lieu of proper training is quite common and unproductive. Use of a training collar can be beneficial when used appropriately but it is not fair to your dog to use as a means of teaching a new behavior. Forcing a dog can create fear and resistance, and have a negative effect on the relationship with your dog. One must be deliberate in how they apply these methods and conscientious of the varying needs of different dogs.

Conditioning a behavior encourages thoughtfulness and creates a positive association. A dog is conditioned by marking a behavior you like with a word like "Good" or a clicker, then giving a reward. Once the dog understands and offers the behavior reliably, you correlate the behavior with a cue. The dogs are actively thinking, developing better learning skills and willingly offering behaviors. This is a force free method of training, can be a slow process, but the learned behavior is deep seeded.

There are a lot of variations to the above methods and a combination generally works best. Most people I work with like the idea of using positive methods but are anxious to eliminate rewards and get impatient with the process. When a dog doesn't immediately respond, there is a tendency to quickly reach in to help or force the dog into a position.

Training is the process of teaching your dog a new language and takes time. We must be clear and consistent, or we create confusion. If you were learning Spanish and the terminology and structure changed daily, you would become confused and likely give up. Before you start teaching this new language, you should be clear with yourself about the cues and responses you are trying to achieve.

We must be patient and allow our dogs time to take in the information, commit it to memory, process and respond. As your dog better understands the cue, the response will become more reliable and come more quickly; however, the cue could include you helping them if you never allow them to think. Some of my training sessions include long periods of waiting, maybe with a foot on the leash or the dog behind a gate, just waiting for them to offer the desired behavior.

If you want a well-behaved dog who can think independently, will offer behaviors and respond without luring, you must give them an opportunity to think. As you transition from luring, work in an area with minimal distractions, give your cue and just wait. Mark and reward incremental progress towards the desired behavior. If your dog gets bored and wanders, use a lead to prevent him from finding entertainment elsewhere. Yes, this is restraint, so remain neutral with the management of the lead, stepping on it is a good way to do that. In the case of an uninterested dog, I will begin with an engagement activity, often an eye contact exercise.

Eye Contact

A simple way to begin teaching eye contact is to sit in a chair with your foot on a lead attached to your dog and a few handy treats. Watch and wait for your dog to glance at you, mark with a word like "Good" and deliver a treat. Once they get the idea that looking at you brings the reward, start adjusting the period of time you reward for the eye contact, counting by seconds in a variable pattern......ex: 1s, 2s, 1s, 1s, 2s, 3s, 1s, 3s jackpot and quit. While the dog is distracted, you are just waiting for the opportunity to capture the look, mark with "Good" and give a reward. You're just sitting and waiting, giving them the opportunity to think and learn on their own that looking at you brings good things.

> TIP: Sometimes, if the dog is really struggling in the beginning, I will adjust my body weight or make a subtle sound to solicit a glance. Be careful not to make this a lure or cue by overusing. We want the dog to think, understand and offer the behavior, so once they get the idea, it is best to patiently wait for an opportunity to reward.

Down

During my most recent writing break, I worked with a six-month pup being trained as Diabetic Alert Dog.   He is very intuitive, owner focused and sweet. He's also very cute and cuddly and likes to suck up next to me when I ask him to down. I am working on extinguishing the luring, so we had a quick two-three minute session on downing. I admittedly cheated by using my German Shepherd, Glacier, to show him the desired behavior.

While the pup sat and processed the cue (and the fact I moved away from him when he tried to schmooze me), I rewarded Glacier for downing. I could see his mind processing the picture. It seemed like an eternity, but it was probably only 20-30 seconds before he downed, quicker than the night before. We tried again with a response time of about 10-15 seconds, then again in about three seconds. We quit with a little party. He was mentally exhausted and ready for a nap after the short session, so I was able to get back to my writing.
Note: You do not need another dog for this process to work, just patience. You can attach a lead to step on while you patiently wait for the down.

Place

We implement a lot of "Place" work in our training practices, using platforms, cots, obstacles and environmental objects like stumps, rocks and manhole covers. We stress the importance of allowing the dog to explore a new obstacle without force and encouraging them to check it out with front feet on before four feet on. We frequently use luring to promote interest, but for an insecure dog, even assertive luring can be too forceful.

Insecure dogs are most negatively affected by force, they need more time to check out an obstacle to assure it is safe. Begin by putting a few treats on the obstacle, take a step back to reduce spatial pressure and allow them to check it out. Reinforce any effort or improvement calmly so you don't startle them. Build confidence on easy obstacles and slowly increase the level of challenge as they are ready. Respect your dog if he is telling you it is too much and absolutely do not try to drag or force him onto an obstacle. Lower your expectations allowing for self-initiated successes to build confidence and develop rational, cognitive thinking.

Take it slow while building a solid foundation and trust. Making big leaps in expectations sets dogs up to fail, potentially scaring or injuring them and ultimately decreasing their confidence. A highly sensitive dog may never recover from a traumatic experience, so it is important to build confidence through success and without force.

Force free training can be applied to all learned behaviors. Once a dog knows how to physically perform a behavior, provide opportunities for them to think and make an association with a cue. Do not be too hasty to reach in and give them help. Set your dog up at a level he can be successful at, stand back and allow him to try. Dogs do what works for them to get what they want. If you hold out for a minute, they are bound to try something they know has worked in the past.

The bottom line......... ***Give your dog time to think.***

Communicating Through Body Language

Dogs are attentive to how we communicate with our body language, expressions and movement. This can be a training advantage or a hinderance depending on the application. Dogs will respond differently depending on the relationship with the individual interacting with them. If your dog trusts you, he will respond much differently towards you than someone he doesn't know or trust.

Many dogs are confused by the controversial way they are approached by strangers. It is very common for someone to see a stunning dog they want nothing more than to approach, pet and snuggle. They walk directly at him staring into his beautiful eyes, tower over top of him while reaching down to give him a pet, or worse a kiss.

Some dogs may not mind but approaching a dog in this manner is a huge gamble. It is very common for a dog to growl or snap when put in this awkward position. An insecure dog will feel very threatened by a domineering approach and if the option to flee is not available, he may bite out of fear. People commonly do not respect a dog's space or understand that these actions are very controversial and can cause discomfort to many dogs.

A dominant or controlling dog may feel challenged by a domineering approach and bite thinking you have no right to intrude in his space, and that you are challenging him.

An insecure dog will respond better to a lowered body posture, diverted gaze and allowing him to approach you on his terms.

Staring directly at a dog can be threatening to a dog. This is different than the soft gaze one might share with their dog or trained eye contact for engagement. Diverting your eyes can help an insecure dog be more comfortable with you.

Towering or bending over a dog is also challenging or threatening to a dog. Lowering your posture and diverting your eyes makes you less threatening and more approachable.

Walking quickly at them is also very unsettling and they may get frightened, feel threatened and react.

When working with your own dog, he will pay attention to your facial expressions, the direction you are looking, the type of look, your reaction to a situation, the position of your body, the direction you are facing, where your shoulders, feet and arms are pointing, your movement and where the reward is.

Your movement influences the motion of your dog. Dogs are drawn to movement, which can be used to motivate a dog to play, to communicate a direction to move in, or trained as commands. If you move away from him, he is inclined follow. If you move towards him, he is inclined to move away. When sending to a place, he will follow your motion or movement towards the object. When waiting at a door he will move back when you step towards him. Quick movements will stimulate a prey driven dog but may cause a more insecure dog to startle, cower, try to flee or bite if he feels trapped.

You can train him to stay in front of you and mirror your movement or follow your hand to teach him to rotate, step forward, backwards and sideways.

You can use spatial pressure to influence your dog's movement and teach wanted behaviors. You can draw your dog towards you by lowering your posture and leaning back or prompt them to move away by stepping towards him. Strategic positioning of your body and movement will result in a variety of responses from your dog, but too much pressure can result in confusion and avoidance behaviors.

Be conscientious of your dog's sensitivity level and focus on building confidence and clarity in what you are trying to achieve. Poor timing, placement or presentation can create confusion, fear and avoidance. Respect your dog's body language and don't be forceful. If he is avoidant give him more space, lower your expectations, take it more slowly and celebrate small successes.

Dogs are very perceptive and pick up on all our bad handling habits. If you reach for your treat pouch during an exercise, they are likely to become distracted by your hand. If you consistently make a movement before releasing, they are likely to break upon your movement. If your movement is jerky and sporadic, he'll be inclined to jump, dart and grab. Be thoughtful in your movement and how you apply it to training.

Everything about you influences your dog. The way you look, how you feel, the tone of your voice, your movements and your reactions to a situation all relay information to your dog. Dogs behave in response to your reactions and how they have been trained. Without guidance, they often respond in undesirable ways. Help your dog make better choices by remaining calm, standing tall, taking charge, staying aware of your surroundings, using trained commands to communicate with him, practicing frequently in various environments and being consistent.

Motivation and Drive

Drive is a set of instinctive behaviors your dog received from his parents. These behaviors are recognizable by their innate impulse to react to certain stimuli. Drive traits are commonly grouped into three categories: Pack, Prey and Defense, and subcategorized into pack, play, food, prey, hunt and defense (fight/flight).

Pack drive refers to behaviors associated with being part of a pack: grooming, play, reproduction, pack hierarchy, licking, mounting and physical contact. Pack drive is relative to their desire to interact with a group. Play drive refers to the desire to engage in entertaining behaviors such as roughhousing, chase games and tug.

Prey drive refers to behaviors associated with hunting: searching, listening, seeing, stalking, chasing, barking, jumping, biting, grabbing, shaking, killing, eating, burying etc. "Hunger is a very primitive and basic drive; without food a canine cannot survive" (Brownell 2). Prey drive is simply the dog's desire to pursue, capture and kill game. Hunt drive is the desire to use their nose to search for prey.

Defense drive is about survival and is divided into fight or flight behaviors. Defense drive is what prompts dogs to protect themselves, their food and their territory from intruders, resistant prey and other dogs. A dog in fight drive will stand tall with hackles raised on the back of the neck and withers, point ears forward, stare directly at opponent and hold an upright stiff tail.

A dog may also defend itself by going into flight mode exhibited by freezing, hiding or running away. They often display hackles along entire neck and back, avoid eye contact and avoid being touched. Dogs in flight mode are likely to bite if the option to flee is removed.

Nerve strength refers to a dog's ability to adapt to stressful stimuli. It is important to work with your dog at a level he can be successful. Be attentive to how your dog handles an environment and adjust your training when needed to create a positive experience that will build confidence. Nerve strength is a highly heritable trait but is also influenced by exposure and socialization throughout their life. Understanding what drives your dog and how he reacts to stimuli will give insight into the best way to interact and reward your dog. Dogs will have various levels of drive within each category. Using play and rewards that are most interesting to your dog will improve your training sessions and relationship with your dog.

When determining drive, we incorporate exercises and general observations to evaluate their level of interest in each area.

Sociability/Pack behavior is apparent by your dog's behavior towards pack members, strange people and strange dogs. This is tested by evaluating the dog's interactions with the handler through play. If the dog disengages, the handler will run away to see if the dog reengages. If he doesn't reengage, the handler will duck in somewhere to hide to see the dog's reaction. Does he come searching or continue about his business? We can test reactions to strangers both human and dog, by back tying and having people/dogs walk by a few feet away to assess his reaction. This can be done with the handler present and out of sight.

Balls and toys can be used to evaluate prey drive. Toss toy multiple times to determine their level of commitment to chasing, carrying and retrieving. A flirt pole (see pg. 104) is a great toy to gauge commitment to chasing, catching and possessing the object. It's also great for building prey and play drive.

Hunt drive can be evaluated by tossing a toy into long grass or bushes to see if he searches until it is found. Scatter feeding kibble in grass, laying short trails using scent pads with treats and setting up enriched exploration exercises are other ways to evaluate hunt and food drive.

Food drive is easy to recognize by your dog's attitude about food and treats. We are often told a dog isn't food driven, but that is rarely the case. Dogs need food and unless they are ill, full, or afraid, they are motivated by food. Dogs who are seemingly unmotivated by food generally have free access to it and have not learned to earn it. Combine this with boring treats, it may seem he isn't food motivated.

PART 2- DEVELOPING HOUSEHOLD AND SOCIAL SKILLS

One way to build the drive for food is to hand feed meals. Another simple way is to use treats your dog perceives as high value, baked hotdogs work well for most. (See "Working for Meals" and "Hotdog Baking Instructions" in Part 1.)

In the Brownell- Marsolais Scale used to evaluate Search and Rescue dogs, nerve strength is determined through tactile, aural and visual testing. Tactile tests include various surfaces both stable and unstable. Aural tests evaluate reactions to loud stimuli such as machinery, yard equipment, gun shots, fireworks, etc. Visual tests expose dogs to moving vehicles and equipment, smoke bombs and other visual stimuli. Above average nerve strength is a very important attribute for working dogs (pg. 5).

There are many tests one can apply to determine their dogs drive, but most behaviors we can observe on a daily basis. Understanding your dog's drive and nerve strength and applying the information to your sessions will help build a more positive association with training and improve the relationship with your dog. Below is a list of traits, used in Wendy Volhard's article, "A Personality Profile for Your Dog," divided into Prey, Pack, Fight and Flight to help you better understand your dog's behaviors.

Pack- Gets along with other dogs, likes people, barks when alone, solicits attention, likes being pet, likes being groomed, seeks eye contact, follows you around, plays with other dogs frequently, jumps on people to greet, mounts other dogs, likes to lick, wants to be with you, attentive to owners, stays aware of your location.

Prey- Sniffs ground and air frequently, gets excited by moving objects, stalks other animals, high pitched bark when excited, pounces on toys, shakes toys vigorously, steals food, gets into garbage, like to carry objects, inhales his food, digs and buries things, likes to chase, runs off after moving objects or animals, puts nose to ground and runs off on an animal trail, sniffs ground and pulls in a direction.

Fight- Stands ground, shows interest in strange objects or sounds, likes to win at tug-o-war, barking or growling in a deep tone, guards his territory, barks at people approaching the home, guards food or toys, dislikes being petted, guards owner, dislikes being groomed, likes to fight with other dogs, got picked on by older dogs when young, barks at other dogs or animals approaching home.

Flight- Runs away from new things, hides behind you, hides during stressful events, acts fearfully in unfamiliar situations, trembles when unsure, whines when stressed, cowers when reprimanded, rolls on back when thinks it's in trouble, reluctant to come all the way when called, avoids eye contact, cowers when someone bends over him, lays down frequently while being groomed, submissive wetting when being greeted, nips or bites when cornered, lays down or rolls on back when confused, any acts of avoidance (pg. 4).

In Volhard's description of how to use the personality profile, she explains that every dog has a varying combination of behavioral traits and will move between pack, prey and defense drive situationally. Drive is not who your dog is, but rather a state of being. Understanding what moves your dog from one state of being to another helps us apply methods and use reinforcement that places your dog in the drive needed for a task.

For most basic commands, your dog needs to be in pack drive to be responsive. Doing something for you such as walking with a loose lead, sitting, downing, staying, coming are all behaviors more easily obtained while your dog is in pack drive. Dogs with many pack drive behaviors will respond to these tasks more readily. Pack drive behaviors are prompted by verbal praise, physical attention, happy facial expressions, grooming and play.

By using treats, toys and movement you can train a dog, with predominately prey driven behaviors, to participate in pack behaviors. Prey drive is drawn out by motions like hand signals, high pitched sounds, objects of value to your dog, chasing, stepping or running away, leaning and moving backward.

Defense drive is important for determining how a dog needs to be trained. Harsh tones of voice, body pressure leaning over the dog, harshly staring at the dog, leash checks and domineering approaches solicit defense drive behaviors.

Dogs can switch from one drive to another in a moment. When you're out for a nice relaxed walk with an attentive dog on a loose leash, they are in pack drive. When a rabbit suddenly runs across your path and the dog reacts by barking and pulling, they are in prey drive. A quick pop of the leash puts them into defense drive, followed up by touch of the head and verbal reinforcement for disengaging with the rabbit puts them back in pack drive. It is your job to figure out what moves your dog from one drive to the next.

In general:

- A dog will need to go through defense drive (our use of body posture, tone or leash check) to get from prey to pack drive.
- A dog will switch from defense to pack drive through smiling, touching and verbal reinforcement.
- A dog will move from pack to prey drive with food, an enticing object and movement.
- A dog with high fight drive will not be bothered much by stern corrections and body language, although conflicting tones and posture will slow down learning. A firm, but pleasant voice should be used.
- A dog with high flight drive will be sensitive to overbearing body language, deep tones and quick movements. Handle gently with calming tones and quiet body movement. Avoid towering overtop, staring directly into eyes, quick movements or hovering. Lower your posture, divert your gaze, allow the dog to approach you and move slowly.
- A dog with high prey drive is easy to motivate with food, toys and movement, but are also easily distracted by moving objects. You will need to be firm when in drive chasing a small animal. Signals and body language will be more effective for training than verbal commands.
- A dog with low prey drive will likely not be easily motivated by food and toys, but also not easily distracted by movement.

- A dog with high pack drive responds well to verbal praise and physical attention. He naturally likes being with you and respond willingly.
- A dog with low pack drive likes to do his own thing and doesn't care about being with his owner. Often found in breeds bred to work independently. You are dependent on using prey drive to train this dog.
- A dog with low prey, low defense and low pack drive will be difficult to motivate, but likely requires little training to be a good pet. Will need a patient trainer for commands because there is not much to work with. These dogs are unlikely to get in much trouble, don't mind being home alone and aren't bothersome.
- A dog with high prey, low pack and low defense drive can be difficult to retain focus on training but is capable if a motivator of interest is used. Training will need to be channeled through prey drive, so a special toy used strategically, or high value treats work best.
- A dog high in prey, low in pack and high in defense(fight) is independent and not the easiest to live with. Excites easily by movement, may be triggered to attack moving objects or anything close and doesn't care much about people or dogs. Professional help is often needed.
- A dog high in prey, low in pack and high in defense (flight) is frightened and startles easily, needs a calm household and a patient, reassuring handler. Not a good choice for a household with children.
- A dog with low prey, high pack and low defense makes an excellent pet. He likes to be with you, rarely gets into trouble, isn't interested in chasing objects and follows well.
- A dog with medium prey, pack and defense (fight) is easily trained and motivated by everything.
- The easiest dogs to train are balanced among all the drives (pgs. 6-11).

The best way to determine what drives your dog is through observation and experimenting. Toss out any preconceived ideas of what you think should motivate him and experiment with different toys, styles of play and treats to see what he enjoys.

Observe your dog's natural behaviors and document your observations over the next several days. Pay attention to the things that excite him, how he interacts and plays with other dogs and people, how attentive he is to you, how much attention he seeks out, tones and sounds he responds to, how he responds to sounds, how he handles new situations and unfamiliar obstacles, his favorite toys, how he likes to play, and which rewards and treats hold the highest value.

Consider how you can apply his favorite things to your interactions and training. If you are working to build drive, reserve his most desired rewards for training purposes. It is difficult to motivate a dog with a reward he frequently gets for free.

Part 2- Developing Household and Social Skills

Potty Training

The Straight Poop- Potty Training Fundamentals
Notes taken from the *Puppy Culture* DVD series.

A separate potty area is important because puppies instinctively want to keep the den clean. It is important for the breeder to keep the litter box and weaning pen clean for health and ease of house training. You want them to be use to keeping their living area clean.

Puppies do not have a lot of control over their bladder and bowels under 12 weeks of age and often don't even realize they need to go. Try to foresee when they will need to go and be prepared with slip on shoes and a jacket near the door. Typically, they'll need to go out about 10 minutes after the start of a play session, 15 minutes after eating, upon waking up, anytime they stop what they're doing and start walking around or sniffing. They will also need to go out at least once an hour during the day.   If they are near the door, take them outside.

When you cannot watch the puppies, put them where they cannot make a mistake. An X-pen attached to a crate for a den with a potty and play area is optimal. Keep the crate door open. Withhold food three hours before and water one hour before bedtime. Take outside immediately before putting to bed. Don't close the crate door until they can go five hours without pottying. Set an alarm to let them out at five hours.

If you catch them in the act of pottying in the house, do not scold. They will perceive they're being scolded for going in front of you and find a safer place to go. They will not want to go in front of you outside either. Don't assume they understand or feel ashamed, they are hiding because they are confused by your behavior. (Killions et. al.)

Crate Training

Crate Games: Start with a large, shallow box or similar objects to teach your dog to go into things. Toss treats into box to develop confidence on an unfamiliar surface, teach them how to enter an object and search. Start implementing a release from the box, a skill that will be implemented in the crate training.

Introduction to Crate

1. Throw cookies towards the back of the crate to get the dog into the crate.
2. Once going into the crate easily, say "Break" to release, then toss a treat outside the crate.
3. Repeat tossing a treat into the crate, once your dog goes in say "Break" before tossing a treat outside the crate. Repeat multiple times.
4. When he turns around inside the crate to face you, ask him to sit or down. Hold for a moment, "Break," toss a treat outside the crate.
5. Repeat several times.
6. Start adding duration by asking to get in position, give a cookie, pause, give a cookie, pause, give a cookie, pause, "Break," toss a treat outside the crate.
7. Repeat multiple times.
8. As the dog improves, start prolonging the pause between treats.
9. Start asking your dog to kennel without tossing a treat in first and reward when he enters.
10. Slowly increase the amount of time before releasing.
11. Start closing the door for a moment, then reopening while he waits.
12. Continue these steps until your dog understands entering the crate without throwing a treat in first, to turn and sit or lay down without a cue and to wait until released.
13. Once he consistently achieves step 12, start closing the door for short periods, staying nearby, dropping treats to reward calm behavior.
14. Start with short time periods, slowly extending the time.

15. Start creating distance by moving away from the crate and returning to reward for calm behavior.
16. Slowing increase the time he spends in the crate and your and distance from it.

TIP 1: A Pet Tutor is a very useful treat dispensing machine that can be attached to the crate and controlled remotely for better timed rewards at a distance.
TIP 2: Food dispensing toys can be used to feed meals in the crate to create a more positive experience.
Tip 3: Crate time is a great time for a tasty chew, frozen stuffed Kong or other long-lasting treat.

Release from Crate

1. Ask your dog to kennel.
2. Close the door while he turns around and wait for him to offer a sit or down. Don't give a command, wait for him to offer the behavior.
3. When he sits or downs, begin to open the door.
4. If he dog gets up, wait for him to sit or down again to actually open the door. This may need to be repeated multiple times before you can open the door without him coming out.
5. Once you get the door open, reward your dog by giving a cookie, pause, give a cookie, pause at least three times before releasing with "Break" and tossing a cookie outside the crate.
6. Add longer pauses with each training session. Reward him for holding his position in the crate once the door is open.
7. Release with "Break" then toss a treat outside the crate.

Comfort Zone- Crate Training and Preventing Separation Anxiety Notes taken from the *Puppy Culture* DVD series.

Structure and structured rest are more important than freedom. Being lose all the time until they become crazy, cranky, mouthy, tired and misbehaved does no one any good. Pups need a place to decompress, so crate training is essential. Breeders should start this by separating puppies for short times during the critical period. The crate becomes a cue to be calm and take a nap. Pups learn to love crate time and are grateful for the break.

Dogs not taught to be alone become upset when isolated and this leads to separation anxiety. They may become destructive and panic. Separation anxiety takes a lot of time and effort to cure. The desire to not be alone is naturally hardwired into dogs. There friendly, social nature is why we were able to domesticate them. If not trained otherwise, they will dread being alone.

Crate training is easy to teach at a young age. Ideally, breeders will leave crates with open doors in a weaning pen. Even without that, they will take to the crate easily if left available. Leave a crate open in the puppy's public area and they will find it.

If they get use to sleeping in a crate with the door open and being away from their siblings, crate training is simple.
To begin crate training, do not feed for a few hours prior and remove water 1-hour prior. Take the puppy out to potty immediately before putting into the crate. Place puppy in the crate with a bone or chew for a few seconds, then open the door and let out before he/she starts fussing. Do an exchange for the bone. Slowly increase the amount of time the puppy is left in the crate, but don't push it. Return to let out of the crate before they wake up and start fussing. (Killion et.al.)

Socialization

Socialization is the process of learning to behave in a socially acceptable way by adapting to the norms of a culture. The process in which we socialize our dogs is a hot topic with contradicting and confusing information. Dog parks have popped up all over and pet parents feel pressured to take their pups out to play for socialization.

I love the idea of the dog park, but in reality, they are dangerous. During a puppy's socialization period, we want to take care that they have positive experiences with appropriate playmates. We see many cases with dogs who have developed reactivity after being attacked at dog parks. We work with fearful owners who have lost a dog due to an attack at a dog park. You have no control at a dog park.

Socialization is not just about getting your dog out to play with lots of dogs and meeting many people. It's much more effective to choose a few appropriate playmates, who are similar in age and play style, with dog savvy owners who understand proper interactions.

Socialization is about getting your puppy accustom to many environments and teaching skills for coping with stress. Give your puppy the opportunity to safely explore as many new places with different surfaces, sounds, smells, people, animals, moving objects, etc. Play with your puppy in these locations putting all the chaos and distractions in the background. Make yourself more fun and valuable than the surroundings.

Do not feel obligated to let people pet your puppy or allow other dogs to approach. If you're not comfortable, say no. Make outings about you and your puppy conquering the environment. It is important for odd things to become the norm for your puppy, but that does not mean they need to interact with everyone.

If you do allow a greeting, pay attention to your puppy's body language and only allow them to go to the person if they are comfortable. Ask the person to crouch down, not reach out at them and only pet if the puppy comes to them. If the other person has a dog, only let them greet if both dogs are acting friendly and manageable. If your dog is cowering, acting stressed or trying to get away, don't force him.

Below, I've included some notes on socialization taken from *Puppy Culture* DVD Series.

Social Graces- Under 12 Weeks

Start training simple foundational behaviors. Recommended skills to begin include recall, walking on leash, sit to ask for things, or manding and crate training.

There are many benefits of early formal training including: Puppies are more likely to benefit rich socialization experiences; Puppies taught with rewards before 12 weeks of age will develop a training relationship that will imprint; As an adult, they will understand training is good and seek out opportunities to work with you.

Early training is easy and your time and energy will pay off big because your puppy will be hungry, socially motivated, attentive to you and it literally only takes one-two sessions to teach the basics.

Running with the Big Dogs- Socialization for Puppies 10-12 Weeks Old

Now that they are vaccinated, meeting lots of safe new dogs in a managed way is important. Dogs use space to control interactions. If they feel pressured or afraid, they will first run away to diffuse the situation. If there is not enough space and they feel cornered, they will turn to aggression to ward off other dogs.

A good set up will have enough space and a way to escape from larger dogs, like a small fence they can squeeze through or low chair. Give the puppy control over the situation so he can build his confidence and overcome fears. This should be done off leash because with a leash on, he can't retreat and it makes him feel defenseless. This is the reason for leash reactivity. A trusted, friendly, adult dog and someone who can read body language is helpful. Give the puppy a safe place and allow him to work out in his own time. Walking with dogs helps them bond and diffuses tension. Do not pay attention or encourage a puppy showing concern, that can reinforce fear. Petting another dog can reassure the puppy. Keep sessions short and give frequent breaks.

Continue challenging puppies during training sessions. Fifteen minutes of mental exercise will tire them out versus hours of physical exercise that will tire them out and they will still be running around biting you.

Dogs don't generalize well. Have your dog meet people of various ages, gender, ethnicity, looks, wearing different things, etc. Expose him to people carrying various objects, pushing/pulling items, creating different movements, engaging in a variety of activity and so on.

Vaccination vs. Socialization- Balancing risks and benefits of early socialization

A little about how vaccines work- If the dam was immune to disease, the puppies will also become immune from the mother's milk. There is uncertainty as to when maternal antibodies wear off. The antibodies generally wear off between six and 14 weeks, in some cases it could be earlier or later. Vaccinations work by modifying a disease so the puppies don't get it, but trick the body into thinking they do so it builds antibodies against the disease. The body will remember how to fight the disease if they are exposed to it again.

If the puppy is vaccinated while he has the mother's antibodies, he will not establish immunity because the mother's antibodies will mask the virus before the puppy's immune system can respond. Three vaccinations are needed because we don't know when the mother's antibodies will wear off and stop interfering with the vaccines. Vaccinations are not recommended under eight weeks because puppies' immune systems are not well established at this age and they would be ineffective. The last vaccination in the series should be given at 16 weeks to be fully effective.

With some precautionary measures, the risk is minuscule that a puppy will come down with disease vs. the high risk of behavior problems without proper socialization.

Bring diverse people and variety of objects into the home. Take extra precautions in the outdoor world. Vaccinate seven days prior to outside exposure. Consider the risk to benefit ratio. Looking at over 1,000 puppies who went to puppy socialization, zero developed Parvo; however, there have been thousands of cases with behavior problem due to lack of early socialization.

A couple of safety guidelines include minimally vaccinating against Parvo and Distemper between seven and eight weeks of age, and seven days prior to exposure. Don't expose your puppy to unvaccinated puppies, dog parks, pet stores, rest stops or other high dog traffic areas. There are no guarantees, but the belief is the benefits outweigh the risks.

Puppy Kindergarten-How to find good one

Puppy classes give opportunity for exposure to a variety of people and dogs. Classes should be structured, predictable, include play, training and relaxation sessions. Transition periods are important to learn at a young age.

When looking for a good class, audit first. Classes should be instructor directed with someone who helps the puppies have a good experience. Instructors should be interactive, stepping in when needed, and matching up puppies with similar play style. They should be able to provide help with other issues.

Play groups should be separated by size, age and play style.

Puppies should be matched up to experience appropriate, reciprocal play. Pups should have places to escape, an environment that shapes confidence, one person for two-three dogs and safe adult trainer dog(s).

There shouldn't be any pig piles, squirt bottles, shake cans, scolding, yelling, pushing pups to play, corrective devices to stop behavior, force or fear tactics. Focus should be on shaping and building positive behaviors.

More is not better; puppies need a lot of rest. When pups are tired, they will start getting snappy and more aroused. After classes, allow them to go home and rest.

A good class agenda will include:
- Sessions transitioning between playing, training and relaxing
- A settling period at beginning of class
- Training exercises like sit, down and calling name
- A play session
- Pass the puppy for treats
- More play
- End with settling and body handling

(Killion et.al.)

Mouthing

Never allow your dog to put its mouth on you, your clothes or leash for any reason. If your dog thinks it is okay to put his mouth on you in play, he will also think it is okay to put his mouth on you when he is scared or angry.

When puppies are among their litter mates, they do lots of mouthing and play-biting. An essential behavior at this age, it helps establish their pecking order and teaches them how hard they can bite before causing pain. It takes them a while to learn what hurts and what doesn't. A dog that is constantly hurting other pack members would cause great turmoil and would ultimately be ostracized or severely corrected.

When a pup comes home with you, he has a history of mouthing behind him. Your family is a new litter; so, instinctively he thinks he has the right to mouth and play-bite again. You and your family must discourage this behavior. Ideally a pup should learn not to mouth you by the time he is twelve weeks old.

Puppies are mouthy and most people think they will simply outgrow it. This is not the case; you need to teach him that it is not proper to put his mouth on people. Look the pup in the eye and say a firm "No." If he is overstimulated or seeking attention, remove the attention and stop the play. If he is tired and persistent, put him away for a nap.

> **Biting- Love Hurts**
> **Notes taken from *Puppy Culture* DVD series.**
>
> Getting a puppy to not bite is a function of how you interact with the puppy.
>
> Don't play in ways that make them crazy or overstimulated. You can't play wild games and expect them not to bite.
>
> Limit the kind of interactions you play with your puppy. Structure interactions that teach him how to properly play in a calm and gentle way. Using intermediary toys to prevent him from biting

your hands is helpful. Hand games invite biting. Calmness is a behavior to be practiced and can be trained like any other behavior. The calmer your interactions are, the calmer he will act and the less he will bite.

If he starts biting, pick him up and turn him away from you. Puppies are biting machines. Keep hands safe by holding the puppy with your hands out of the way. Hold him and gently massage until calms. This technique is less about correcting and more about avoiding.

Movement is a cue to bite. If he bites while walking or running, stop moving. Use food and praise to reinforce walking next to you without biting.

Stop playing and give the puppy a break before he becomes over tired and starts getting mouthy.

Biting kids is not about dominancy. The definition of dominant is in control of resources, children have more access to resources than dogs. Children interact in excited ways and react in a stimulating way when the puppy bites. Work with the kids and puppy to have calm interactions.

Managing Biting- Yelping and rolling the lip can amp the dog up more. You may need to put the puppy away if the biting can't be managed. Management strategies may include prying off object, pick up facing away from you, put away for a break or have training session marking and rewarding for walking nicely without biting. It is a judgement call if you should work on training or just manage the behavior at the time. You may not be able to play all the games you want. If you manage the biting for the first month or two, he will grow out of it and it will have a positive impact on your relationship for the life of the puppy. (Killion et.al.)

Resource Guarding

Guarding of food, chew items, toys or stolen items can pose a huge concern. Many dog owners have been bit trying to retrieve a paper towel or tissue their dog has stolen out of the garbage or off a table. It's not uncommon for a dog to growl over a bone, their food or even their space.

Resource guarding can be very difficult to fix unless addressed before twelve weeks of age. We have a much better chance for success during the socialization period. Anti-resource guarding protocol should be added to all training programs before twelve weeks of age. We need to teach our dogs that our approaching them brings good things. If you are having issues with resource guarding, you need to seek help from a trainer for special instructions.

Everything Here is Mine
Notes taken from *Puppy Culture* DVD series.

It is natural for puppies to guard food. If they didn't, they would starve in a wild setting. They learn to communicate ownership of resources and avoid conflict by respecting each other's possessions.

Why do dogs resource guard? It is a normal, legitimate behavior to guard possessions. Humans don't respect dog's ownership of resources and believe they should give them up. This is unnatural to dogs and must be taught.

There is a learning moment when a dog first acts possessive. You can snatch it away now, but when they get older and stronger, they may bite. Instead, quickly replace the object with something great, so the puppy begins to feel happy when you take things away. Train with high value, puppy appropriate objects, trade for a high value treat, then give the original object back. Do this over and over so puppy perceives your reaching in as a good thing.

Doing exchanges with all young puppies to avoid resource guarding has high success. This is best done at six-eight weeks.

The opportunity is lost by twelve weeks. It is recommended for dog breeders and puppy owners to work anti-resource guarding protocol for all puppies under twelve weeks of age in the following four areas:

Food Dish- Add food to the dish while the puppy is eating. Use something tastier than what is in the dish. We want to develop CER (Conditioned Emotional Response)- a happy reaction when you approach. Exchange the dish for a treat. Don't hold treat out as bribe, rather keep it hidden as you approach. Walk up, take the dish away, then offer the treat.

Objects- Exchange an object for a new object. Take the object away, give a payoff, then give the object back. Use a variety of toys and chews. Repeat. Incorporate touching the puppy before the exchange, because some may object to that as well.

Sleeping Locations- Approach the puppy when sleeping in comfy location, give a treat and leave. To prevent lap guarding with small dogs, approach while they are being held and give a treat.

Touchy, Feely Body Handling- People understand hugging and touching as affection, dogs do not naturally understand that. This can be learned. The earlier the start the better. Breeders should be handling and touching from the time they are born. As they age body handling should be continued, but their social need decreases. Start rewarding for touch by touching a paw, rewarding, touching an ear, rewarding, etc. Keep the food out of sight of the puppy so as not to frustrate him.

Positive reinforcement releases dopamine in the brain increasing the bond between dog and owner.

Punishment activates the fear system and can have negative effects. It can illicit an aggressive response in dogs from a simple leash correction or yelling NO. (Killion et.al.)

Part 3- Pack Structure and Leadership

Pack Structure

The familiar scent of white-tailed deer drifted over the six wolves as they rested in a small stand of scrub pines. The dominant female was the first to notice. She opened her eyes, raised her head, and sniffed the air, languidly at first, then with interest. As she rose, the dominant male, or "Alpha," opened his eyes and looked at her. He sampled the scent drifting through, then slowly rose. Quietly, the other wolves, two juveniles and two low-ranking females, made their way over to the dominant male, all stopped and turned into the wind, toward the deer. They came together, touched noses, and slowly headed toward the deer, the dominant male in the lead.

The wolves quietly approached a snow-covered clearing in the woods. Small plants broke the surface of the shallow snow in places. Two deer fed on the plants and on lichen growing on the trunk of a young scrub pine. One of the deer stopped, looked up, then continued feeding. At that moment the Alpha male sprung into the clearing, running full speed almost instantly. The dominant female leapt into the clearing from the opposite side, accompanied by the other four wolves. A fifth deer saw the Alpha male first and turned to flee, realizing their mistake too late. The dominant female closed the distance and jumped onto the back of the smaller deer, quickly joined by one of the juvenile males and the Alpha male. The deer was quickly brought down and killed. The other wolves gave chase to the surviving deer, but quickly withdrew, too excited by the fresh kill.

The Alpha male ate the deer's tongue, while the dominant female tore into the animal's hindquarters. They allowed the juveniles to join in, but when the two low-ranking females came too close, the Alpha male snarled them back. He would allow them to feed only after he, his mate, and the juveniles had fed sufficiently. The low-ranking females backed away, yipping in protest and hunger. After a few minutes, they again carefully approached. This time the leader allowed them to feed on the carcass. In an hour, the pack had consumed most of the deer. They lay close to each other;

cleaning themselves. Satisfied, they would rest for a few minutes and then return to their favorite place a half-mile into the forest, where they would sleep, play and celebrate their good luck. The Alpha male would lie quietly in his favorite place, a high spot near an old Jack pine. He would watch the others and think of how much the young ones had learned in such a short time. (Baer and Duno xi-xii)

Naturally, all animals including humans have a pecking order. Any herd, flock, pack or group of animals has an alpha and omega with a complex social group in between. The natural pecking order system can be quite harsh among the animals, fights to the death are not unusual.

Animals all instinctively understand body language. They know big, tall and puffed up looks dominate and is something to be reckoned with. Whether a rooster in the chicken yard or a dog at the dog park, it means the same thing. Stern eye contact can be a dominate challenge. Looking away, lowering the body posture and tail shows submission.

Since we are addressing dogs in this book, we will be referring to the pack. We will often make reference to the wolves because they are closely related to domestic dogs. We see the same basic behavior patterns in our pet Chihuahua as in a wild pack of wolves.

The leader of a pack has a lot of responsibility. Leaders control space, territory, food, breeding, where and when the pack goes out for a hunt, sleeping place and the safety of the pack. The rest of the pack needs to be confident that the leader will protect them and be a fair, reliable, consistent leader.

I can't stress enough how important it is for pet owners to be the leader of their pack in order to keep safety and harmony in the household.

The intent of this section of the book is to provide a basic understanding of the behaviors canines exhibit when establishing leadership and vying for their position in the pecking order. The genetic traits dogs carry on from their wild ancestors will vary among breeds and individuals, but they are still very relevant to the relationship you have with your dog.

PART 3- PACK STRUCTURE AND LEADERSHIP

You don't have to exhibit physical strength to show you're the pack leader. Dogs don't care how strong you are, they are looking for the signs of leadership such as: Who's leading the way? Who's controlling the food? Who gets the best sleeping place? Who does the dog feel safe with?

Why is it so important for you to be the leader of your dog pack?

Some people have stated they don't care if their dog runs the household. Some think it is cute and funny to have their small dog take charge. It is rare a dog will be tolerable to live with without structure and boundaries. Often dogs placed in the position of leadership become very dominant, controlling and sometimes aggressive. A less confident dog may become fearful and anxious with potential to bite or nip out of fear. Allowing your dog freedom to establish leadership can create a dog who is dangerous living in our society. Once a dog has taken on the leadership role, it is very difficult to reestablish yourself as the leader. Most dogs don't want the leadership job. The leadership role places a lot of stress on a dog who doesn't want the position.

The leader of the pack has three very important jobs. One of the leader's jobs is to **discipline the pack**. If your dog runs the house, he will feel obligated to give a correction by growling, snapping or even biting if anyone does anything deemed wrong. Disturbing your dog when he is resting, trying to take something away from him, grooming when he doesn't want to be groomed are actions your dog may deem correctable behaviors.

The leader additionally has the responsibility of **protecting the pack**. You may think this is good because you want protection. Unfortunately, without training and boundaries, dogs don't always use the best judgment determining when protection is needed. Unwanted bites occur very commonly when dogs feel they need to protect themselves and their pack. A friend may suddenly come into your house unannounced and your dog bites this intruder. While your kids are play wrestling with their friends, your dog thinks they are in trouble and bites. Your dog may have a strong desire to take control of situations and will often bark and lunge as strangers approach.

PART 3- PACK STRUCTURE AND LEADERSHIP

The leader of the pack **controls the food and other resources**. The Alpha eats first allowing the rest of the pack to eat on his terms. Possessions are turned over to the leader at his will. This can cause a lot friction in people's homes.

Dogs control possessions by running away, hiding, holding tight with mouth and feet, hovering, guarding, growling, snapping and biting. Possessive aggression is demonstrated when growling, snapping and biting occur. This is a very dangerous type of aggression! It is highly unlikely that possessive aggression can be extinguished completely unless the puppy is under twelve weeks old. We have successfully changed this behavior in puppies, but we have never seen this behavior permanently corrected when addressed over twelve weeks of age. On-going training and management of this aggressive behavior becomes the only option and comes with risk.

It is important to provide your dog with good leadership and structure. It can be detrimental to allow your dog to take control of your household.

Anyone who has doubts that our pet dogs still carry the traits of their wolf ancestors should watch the "White Wolf" video from National Geographic. It is about a pack of wolves living in the Arctic who have never seen humans before. You will see all the same traits in the wolves that you see in our personal, domestic dogs. The wolf pack's behaviors and skills are about survival. Pet dogs don't need all these skills to survive, but they still have the instincts to exhibit these behaviors. They can't just turn off their natural instincts even if they are no longer needed. In our society many of these traits are considered behavior problems and people work hard trying to correct them.

A few of the instinctual behaviors you will recognize in the video are:

- The pack leader prefers to sleep in a high place so he can keep an eye on the surrounding area.
- The pack has a structured hierarchy.
- They dig holes to have a warm comfortable place to sleep or to bury possessions.

- They make noise if an outsider approaches to alert the pack to possible danger.
- They fight for, beg and steal food or else they would die of starvation.
- They enjoy grooming and rubbing, but only on their terms.
- They discipline improper behavior.
- The pack demonstrates the same body language as domestic dogs.
- The pack enjoys stealing, chase and keep away games.
- The pack is very territorial. Strangers are not tolerated in their territory.
- They chase, grab, shake, kill and eat their prey.

Leaders Eat First

Anyone who has watched a documentary on the wolf pack has witnessed how aggressively the wolves take control of their food. The dominant wolves eat first while the omega wolves wait anxiously to be allowed their turn to eat. They eat quickly and stand on guard to defend their food from anyone coming too close. You can hear the evil sounds of growling and snarling. There is tension in the entire pack. Dinner at the wolf den is nothing like Thanksgiving dinner in a human house.

Wolves have to work for their food. They hunt for it, carry it to a safe place to eat and vie for their turn to partake in the eating of the kill. They do not have regular times every day that they get their food handed to them. They eat large, infrequent meals versus small meals two to three times a day.

Often owners expect our canine companions to come into their house fully understanding what the rules are at mealtime. A confident, food driven dog will instinctively dive into the food. When it's your dog's turn to eat, insist he works for his food by doing something to earn it. Earning their food could be as simple as "sit and stay," as complex as "go get your dish," or a series of behaviors.

Handle the Dog's Food Bowl

In the quest to teach their puppy not to be aggressive over food, owners can unintentionally cause the pup to have food aggression. While it's true owners have the right to take the dogs food away without any growling, snapping or biting, it's the way this is taught that can create a problem.

Aggression can be created by taking the dog's food away repeatedly. A common example of how this can happen follows: The owner works with the dog to establish food control by removing the dog's food. The dog starts to get annoyed and gives a little growl of frustration. The owner hears the growl and doesn't give the food back right away. The food is returned for a moment, then taken away again. The dog becomes more serious with a firmer growl. The owner corrects the dog and refrains from giving the food back right away. After a period of time, the owner gives the food back and proceeds to take it again. This time the dog is so frustrated, he snaps at the owner. The owner now corrects the dog harsher and does not return the food. Now everyone is tense at mealtime and the situation gets worse. The dog doesn't trust the owner and the owner doesn't trust the dog.

The dog growls or snaps because he is worried you will take his food away and the behavior is reinforced each time you do. Guarding food is important for survival. They would not survive in the wild if they allowed someone to take their food away. You don't want your dog to think you are going to be unfair by taking his food away, you want your dog to get excited when you approach his dish.

To get your dog used to you handling his food, start off by feeding him food from your hand. Add food or drop special treats to his dish while he's eating. Give him a little pet while adding something special to the meal. Remain calm and relaxed while doing this.

Food aggression can be created by feeding three or more small meals a day instead of one or two larger meals. Dogs are not grazers; they like to feel full at least once a day. Small meals can frustrate a large dog because they never get the satisfaction of feeling full and satisfied.

Feeding one large meal each day and a snack or treats throughout the day will help them feel more satisfied and satiated. If weight is a problem, soak the food in water, add low calorie vegetables, or use a high-quality canned food. The quality dog kibble is so concentrated, that dogs don't get to eat much before reaching their calorie limit for the day. Canned food does not have near the calories per cup that the kibble has, so it can aid your dog in losing weight without feeling like he is starving.

Warning signs of food aggression:

- The dog tenses up if he is touched while eating.
- The dog stops eating and hovers over his dish if someone approaches while he is eating.
- The dog growls if someone comes near, touches food, dish or dog while he is eating.

- The dog snaps or bites if anyone gets near his food or dish while he is eating.
- The dog guards his dish even if there is no food in it and he is not eating.

If your dog exhibits these behaviors, contact *A Canine Experience, Inc.* for instructions on feeding food aggressive dogs.

Leaders Go First

The pack was on the move, looking for food. They had scented the recent passage of a group of mule deer, but the scent was weakened by a late storm that deposited six inches of new snow in the valley. Three days had passed since the last kill and the Alpha knew he needed to lead his pack to something soon.

The end of the valley narrowed into a tight gorge with high, eroded sandstone walls. The trees here were sparse, mostly larch and a few young aspens. Most of the ground was choked with thick stands of wild blackberry and dwarf pines. The Alpha led the pack along a slim trail that wound through the thorny blackberry bushes and headed for a narrow pass regularly used by deer to enter and exit the valley. It was tight going. The pack had to travel single file to avoid getting pecked by thorns, the Alpha went first, closely followed by his mate and their five-month-old pups, a male and a female. Behind them were two subordinate males, three-year-old females, and an older lone female who had been loosely accepted by the pack a week before.

Once out through the pass, the Alpha immediately picked up scent in the area near a small pool of water and found fresh deer droppings, no more than 10 minutes old. Each wolf in turn sniffed at the droppings, then followed on, excited and confident that soon their leader would locate the deer.

One of the subordinate males picked up the scent of a female mule deer in heat and in his excitement, bounded ahead of the pack. The Alpha was not pleased with this; the young male was not as experienced at tracking and could very well spook the deer, ruining the chances for a successful hunt. He quickly and silently snapped out at the young male as he went by, then forced him off the trail into some loose sandstone.

The Alpha then jogged back to the head of the procession and continued tracking the female mule deer, who was now very close. The young male, no worse for the incident.

After they fed on the old female mule deer, the wolves rested and groomed each other. The young male, sleepy from the large meal, quietly lay down a few yards from the Alpha. The leader rose, walked over to the young male and stood next to him, pawing slightly at the ground. They licked each other's faces and joined the rest of the pack for a well-earned sleep. (Baer and Duno 54-55)

Picture a wolf pack walking through the woods, you'd immediately recognize the canine in front as the leader. The Alpha leads the pack to their destination, sets the pace and determines when they will stop. The leader will mark their territory as they move through the area.

Domestic dogs love going for walks. It is in their nature to explore their territory while sniffing, marking and running. These activities are all very exciting to a dog and most dogs leap for joy when they see their leash come out. Many owners struggle to get the leash attached as their dog tosses its body about leaping at the door while barking. Once wrestled down and the leash is attached, the lunging and barking continues. To stop the commotion, the owner opens the door and lets the dog charge out in a crazy frenzy. Does this sound familiar?

The leader of the wolf pack or even a domestic dog pack would not allow the subordinate dogs to go out in front of him and will correct them for acting up. This is the reason many dog fights happen at doors and gates. When two or more dogs are excitedly going out the door, one will step in and correct the other dog for trying to go first. Often the correction is given unfairly due to overstimulation, the other dog reacts in protest and a fight breaks out. Dogs act differently in a heightened state of arousal than they normally would.

Owners usually think of a walk as the dogs treat, so they allow the dog to control the walk. The dog pulls ahead, sniffing, marking, going slow, going fast, wrapping the leash around the handler's legs and stopping to sniff while the owner patiently waits. Giving freedom to sniff and explore should be on your terms, they should still heed to leash pressure and return when called. Practice moving from a controlled walk, to allowing exploration and back to controlled. It's important you can tighten up your walk quickly when needed.

To get the most benefit and enjoyment from your walk:

- Make your dog sit and wait while you put the leash on.
- Teach your dog to wait to go out the door until after you have gone through. Let your dog know when it's okay to come through by using a release word like "Okay," "Free" or "Release."
- Every time you go through an outside door or gate, insist that your dog waits, and you go through first. Eventually, your dog will get the point and just start letting you go first.
- Your dog should walk politely at your side, adjusting his pace to match yours and stopping when you do.
- Give your dog a release command like "Go Sniff" or "Check it Out" when it is okay to explore and have more lead.
- Practice having your dog return to you for a treat and release back to exploring.
- Take working walks by adding in turns, auto sits, downs, stays, obstacles, up, over, through under, weaves, places, etc.
- Make it fun, use the environment as your obstacle course. Be creative.
- Do not allow your dog to mark out its territory on your walk. Stop and give your dog a potty breaks and time to explore, but do not allow him to wet on everything he smells along the way.

The waiting exercise should make a lot of sense to your dog and they generally figure it out quickly. If "Wait" is a new behavior for your dog, it will take some persistence to teach him the new rules. Be consistent with your expectations to create clarity with your dog.

Leaders Control Space

The Alpha male suns himself in the center of a small alpine meadow, savoring the warmth of the afternoon sun. A subordinate female leisurely grooms him, chewing and licking at parasites embedded in his hindquarters. He is grateful and she feels at ease with him.

A two-year-old subordinate male trots over, circles the resting pair, then casually plops down next to the female. The Alpha male lifts his head, looks straight at the young male and lets out a low, almost inaudible growl, his lips pulled back ever so slightly from his teeth. He doesn't bother getting up. The female goes back to her grooming.

The young male's ears are sat back against his head, but he doesn't move. The Alpha continues his stare, now fully bearing his fangs. The young male averts his gaze, gets up slowly, and walks away, saving face and perhaps a bit more.

After a few minutes, the Alpha male gets up and shakes off, ending the grooming session. He gives the female a lick of appreciation and then trots over to where the rest of the pack is resting, playfully charging into the group and circling them quickly. The others get up and join him, romping and chasing him around the meadow, enjoying the last rays of the afternoon sun. (Baer and Duno 13)

When the leader of a wolf pack walks through, his pack will move out of his way, because they respect his space. If the leader is laying down resting, subordinates will carefully walk around him. This is different than many of our domestic dogs who will walk right over their owner if resting on the floor. If someone lives with a large dog who is blocking their path, the owners will often walk around the dog rather than making the dog move out of their way.

If your dog is sleeping peacefully on the sofa where you want to sit, do you carefully sit beside your dog so you don't disturb his sleep or do you

make the dog move out of your way?
If your dog is laying in the middle of your kitchen floor while you are cooking dinner, do you keep stepping over him or walk around him, or do you make him get up and leave the kitchen?

Does your dog often bump or step on you (including your feet) and you assume it is accidental?

Your dog knows exactly what he's doing. He is testing your space to see what he can get away with. These simple actions communicate to your dog that they control the space.

You may think your dog is just being affectionate when he leans on you, but that is not always the case. Many dogs lean on people in an effort to control them.

Dogs should respect the owner's space. Many dogs use their bodies as a way to control space by blocking, leaning, jumping, stepping on, sitting on, pawing at, etc. Your dog should move out of your way if he is blocking your path or if he is on the furniture and you want to sit down. If he doesn't move, say "Move" and walk toward him gently guiding him out of your way. If he growls or displays any aggression when you make him move, he lacks respect and you should seek professional help.

Many dogs have learned how to get their owners to pet them by bumping their hand with their nose, pawing at the hand with their foot, leaning on them or climbing into their lap. These are all ways they use their body to control their owners. Most owner's instant reaction is to oblige their dog by petting without a thought as to how they have allowed them to take control.

Any owner whose dog is exhibiting behavior problems needs to pay close attention to the ways their dog is challenging them. Petting and attention should be given on your terms. If your dog approaches you soliciting attention, have him do something to earn the petting. Asking your dog to sit or lie down is a good way to turn his controlling you into you controlling him.

You do not have to pet your dog for complying with your request after he solicits attention. A sit or down can be turned into a duration exercise or he can be sent to his bed or place.

In your dog's quest to control his space, he may act aggressively when being walked on a leash. This aggression occurs when a strange dog or person approaches by putting on a good show and acting as scary as he can. This stresses the owner, who tightens up the leash and hangs on with all his/her strength. The approaching person will generally keep their distance and leave the area. The aggressive act worked for the dog, now everyone is calm, and the dog saved the pack from harm. Next time an intruder approaches, he will try to act more vicious, the owner will become more stressed, reinforcing the behavior more each time.

Proper training can easily break the cycle of reactivity on leash. When the leader remains calm and confident while using the dog's obedience, the situation can be defused with most dogs.

When your dog starts showing interest in an approaching dog or person, you can redirect him in a number of ways. It is important to communicate with your dog before they are overstimulated and to keep tension off the leash. Watch your dog's body language and redirect when you notice them stare, tense up or start to drive forward towards a trigger. You can ask him to sit, down or go to a place, then work to gain eye contact. Another great strategy is to move your dog away from a trigger by moving away, prompting him towards you and tossing a treat past your body. The objective is to reward him for moving away from the person or dog rather than growl, bark or lunge.

How you proceed will depend on the aggression history of your dog. If you trust your dog is safe and has no history of aggression, you can allow the person to calmly pet him. If you don't trust your dog, he is unstable or has a history of aggression, you may have the person drop a treat on the ground for him. Don't force your dog to greet or be pet by people. Allow your dog to approach the stranger only as he becomes comfortable. Do not allow the person to approach your dog if he is acting aggressive or fearfully.

Sessions using exploration with stimulus present at a distance are very beneficial. Allow your dog to slowly decrease the distance in a wandering pattern as he becomes comfortable. Do not allow the dog to move straight towards the stimulus. Stop him slowly or prompt a U- turn if he moves forward too quickly. It is important not to push the dog beyond his comfort level provoking an aggressive or fearful response. Call ACE for guidance using acclimation and exploration methods.

Leaders Sleep in Highest, Softest, Most Desirable Place

It is important for a leader to protect his territory. In doing this, they prefer to rest in an area where they can see their surroundings, so higher is better. You may have noticed that your dog loves being up on the furniture. Sure, it is comfortable, but mainly it is higher. Often the sofa is not high enough, they want to be up on the back of the sofa. Owner's beds are their favorite.

Allowing your dog to sleep in the bed may give them the perception they own and have the right to control the bed. **Allowing your dog to sleep in your bed can cause huge behavior problems!** I know that many people don't want to hear this, but it is so true! Even the most-mild mannered dog can start displaying aggressive behaviors when allowed to sleep in the owner's bed. We have seen this over and over again.

We've worked with many dogs who had never shown any aggressive behaviors until the owner started letting them sleep on the bed. The owners first noticed a little growl when they were disturbed while sleeping on the bed. It starts with just a little grumble, but if left unchecked the growl would turn into a snap and eventually someone gets bit.

Some examples of aggressive behavior I've worked with include: Dogs who have attacked children in the middle of the night because the child bumped the dog while he was sleeping on the bed; Dogs would not allow the owner to return to the bed after getting up to use the bathroom; A dog who bit the owner because she tried to make the bed in the morning before the dog was ready to get up; and several dogs who would not allow children to come to the parent's bed at night.

I've known countless people who were rushed to the emergency room because they disturbed their dog while he was asleep. These are not isolated cases; it can easily get this bad if the dog is allowed to continue staying on the bed if he growls when someone bumps or moves him.

I had a very well trained, friendly dog that really enjoyed the special treat of occasionally cuddling on my bed with me. When she was in this special place, she would suddenly become vicious if my other dog, a very dominant male who she greatly respected, would come near the bed. She would never consider showing any aggression toward him any other time, but on my bed, she acted very bold and confident. She even growled at my husband and daughter if they touched her while on the bed with me. I quickly followed my own advice, never allowed her cuddle time on the bed again and she never showed this aggressive behavior again. You can put a dog bed on the floor next to your bed for him to sleep on. If you can't keep your dog out of your bed, you may need to have him start sleeping in a crate.

I am not saying that every dog that sleeps in the owner's bed will eventually bite them. If you are having behavior problems or your dog shows any aggression at all, you need to keep him off the bed and all the furniture. Dogs who are allowed full freedom of your bed, furniture and lap will be less respectful of your space.

To teach your dog to stay off the furniture, leave a light leash on your dog. Use the lead to help guide your dog off the furniture while telling him "Off." Our goal is to teach your dog to remove himself from the furniture when you tell him "Off." You can also toss treats to the floor while saying "Off." Do not grab his collar and pull him off, this can result in a bite or avoidance behaviors. If a dog is used to having free run of the furniture and you suddenly grab his collar and pull, he may swing and snap at you.

This does not mean you can never have your dog in your lap or cuddle with him, but these should only be allowed on your terms. Invite your dog up when desired and ask your dog to get off when you're ready. Do not allow him to jump on and off your lap at will!

Do not allow your dog to remain in your lap if he demonstrates aggressive behavior towards other people or pets. Growling or snapping as people approach is generally a sign your dog is being possessive and feels he owns your lap. Have him get off and ask him to sit or down. Do not allow the approaching person or animal to force themselves on your dog, it is your job to protect him while demonstrating you're in charge.

Leaders Don't Chase

One of the young members of the pack grabs a large stick and proceeds to taunt the rest of the pack, proudly flaunting his precious possession. He tosses it about in an attempt to entice the others into playing his favorite game of catch me if you can. The Alpha male and older wolves don't even look his way, they would never stoup to chasing a subordinate. He finally succeeds at coaxing a group of young wolves to chase him. They annoyingly run through the camp, twisting, turning and recklessly jumping over some of the resting pack.

The Alpha, tired of their disrespectful nonsense, approaches the juveniles giving a quick snapping growl. The young wolf stops, drops the stick, puts his tail down and saunters off. He was only temporarily discouraged, the next day he would play his favorite chase game again. (Baer 21)

Playing with your dog is very important in the development of your relationship. Dogs don't distinguish the difference between playing, working and general manners. We need to be consistent with our rules and boundaries during play, work and while just hanging out. If we allow mouthing, running from you playing catch me games and jumping on you during play, they will not understand it isn't appropriate at other times.

Many people misunderstand the role of canine play. Running, shaking, jumping, tugging, chasing and biting are skills a canine would need to hone for survival in the wild. The fastest, strongest, most physically coordinated canine would be the most likely to climb the ladder of hierarchy and become the leader. While our pets do not need these skills for survival, those instincts remain intact at various levels.

We often hear comments such as:
"We are just playing."
"I don't mind if my dog puts his mouth on me. He is gentle about it."
"I let my dog jump on me and grab my sleeve when we are playing."

"I love to chase my dog around the back yard when he has his ball."

"I chase him to try to get his toy back."

"I chase and corner him to retrieve stolen items."

"I love to wrestle with my dog and let him climb all over me."

These are phrases we hear frequently associated with behavior problems. You cannot separate play from the rest of your dog's behavior. We want to engage in games that are constructive, not destructive.

Chasing can lead to a dog who plays catch me games when you need to leash him up or who will only come on his terms. If he tries to engage you in a chase game, don't chase him. You need to become exciting as you move away from him or stop your interaction and remain neutral. Don't get angry and use a gruff voice, that makes you unapproachable. Use coming games to create a positive association with coming. Play engagement games to develop a dog who comes to you to interact, rather than entertain themselves by running from you.

Chasing and cornering a dog to recover a toy or stolen object can trigger possessiveness and they sometimes respond by growling, snapping or lunging. We want to avoid putting our dogs in a position to fail.

Dogs will at times challenge you during these games and we want to be sure to have clear, consistent, respectful rules. If your dog is mouthing or jumping on you, they are being rude, and the game should stop.

Leaders Display Dominant Posturing

The Alpha male lazily warms himself in the afternoon sun while two 4-month-old pups play-wrestle with each other close by. He watches them stalk, jump and then chase each other around an old Douglas fir. Their play spills over into the Alpha's resting place, but they are having too much fun to notice. One of the pups, suddenly decides to include the Alpha in the game. He jumps up at the Alpha's throat and mouth, biting and pawing at him, trying to goad him into play. The Alpha easily and calmly pins the pup down with one front paw, grabs him around the throat with his powerful jaws and gently holds him, all the while growling softly. The pup rolls over on his back and from that position licks the Alpha's face. The Alpha returns the lick and walks away.

All the pups then run over to a juvenile female who has been watching. She goes into play posture and goads the pups into chasing her around a large boulder. After a few minutes, she tires of the game and walks away from the pups who try to keep the game going for a bit but then give up. They stop for a moment wondering what to do next. Then the dominant pup runs off quickly, the other one hot on his trail. (Baer and Duno 36)

Animals, including humans, are strong at reading body language. If someone tells you he/she is happy yet is slouched in a chair with a sad face, will you believe what the person says or what the body language is telling you? I have studied the body language of many species of animals and found they are very similar.

If you study a wolf pack, you will quickly recognize which are acting dominantly and which are more submissive by watching their body language. When interacting with a challenging member of the pack, the leader will stand up straight and tall with his tail held high and stiff, chest puffed up and neck arched over the neck of the other wolf. The opposing wolf has the choice of challenging the alpha wolf causing a fight or lowering his posture with ears laid back and tail tucked indicating he is giving in to the dominant wolf.

If you have watched dogs interact at a dog park, I am sure you have seen these behaviors many times. When you enter a dog park with your dog, this happens over and over as the dogs at the park work out the pecking order for the day. The problem arises when two dominant dogs both want to be in charge. Very often the dogs will work it out themselves by posturing, growling and sometimes a scuffle. People usually panic, blaming one of the dogs for being aggressive. Some are truly aggressive, overbearingly dominant or lack social skills, but often they are communicating in "Dog Language" and will work it out on their own if given the opportunity. It really isn't natural for dogs to go to the same places everyday and meet a different group of dogs each time. There is a lot of work in figuring out the hierarchy for the day. The younger dogs are eager to show their submission so they can get on with the play. Mature dogs are much more serious about establishing their dominance and taking control of the park.

So how does all this posturing relate to your relationship with your dog? Your dog looks at your posture to see if you are the dominant one. Asking your dog to respond to your requests while you are bending down into a submissive posture is less effective than asking while standing up straight in a dominant posture. Your dog will be more responsive if you stand up straight while giving the command. It will take practice to get your dog listening while in a lowered position.

Lying on the floor and allowing your dog to stand over you sends the wrong message to your dog. If kids are sitting on the floor and your dog hovers over them, it is important to step in and remove the dog from the position. Dogs often need help understanding they cannot be dominant over children and most children need help managing the dog.

Body language is not always easy to read because the same body movement doesn't always mean the same thing. For example, if a dog lays its ears back it could mean it's afraid, submissive, nervous, enjoying play or wanting to be pet. Tail wagging can be a sign of happiness, nervousness, submissiveness or even aggression. It really depends on the way the dog is moving his tail and what the rest of his body is doing.

Many people have misread a dog by thinking because the tail is wagging, he must be friendly. A dog wagging his tail low with fast, short wags may be nervous and/or submissive. A dog wagging his tail with high, long, relaxed wags is usually happy. A high, stiff tail with short wags can be dominant and/or aggressive.

A dog rolling over on its back can also be misunderstood. It can mean the dog is submissive or the dog loves to have his belly rubbed. Very dominant dogs may roll over to encourage someone to rub its chest and take advantage by hitting you with his feet. Again, taking control of the interaction.

Drooling can have different meanings also. Some dogs drool in anticipation of something good to eat, other times they are nervous or don't feel well.

Body language is a very effective way for you and your dog to communicate. Dogs take notice of multiple points on your body: where your eyes are looking, direction your body is facing, posture, movement of your limbs, facial expressions, movement of your body, direction of movement, speed of movement, hardness/softness of eyes and direction of shoulders and toes.

Additionally, dogs are sensitive to your emotions, your smells and your tone of voice. The smell of your body chemistry changes with adrenaline, medical conditions, medications, etc. - therefore, it can be really difficult to fake out a dog if you are fearful or anxious. All these things matter to your dog and if he senses you're not strong or stable, he's more likely to try to take control or become fearful and anxious.

Leaders Remain Calm and Fair

The pack rested after eating. The young elk had been taken down by three young males after they discovered it limping across the muddy flood plain of a small alpine lake. By the time the rest of the pack arrived, the three were busily eating.   The Alpha male sauntered over to the kill, sniffing and licking at it while the three young hunters watched, momentarily halting their feeding not sure if they should surrender their hard-earned privilege. Then, the Alpha male walked off a few paces and lay down, content to watch the three fledgling hunters enjoy their first kill together.

The rest of the pack tentatively joined the three young males, who by now had each eaten close to their fill. The Alpha male came over to join in on the meal. He was impressed at the size of the juveniles' first kill and at their initiative. To show his respect, he had allowed these three first-feeding privileges. Confident in his leadership, he knew that they would not interpret his acquiescence as weakness, but rather as tribute to their success. It was the fair thing to do.

The leader of a wolf pack is not a tyrant, but rather a benevolent dictator and an efficient administrator: He should not steal from a subordinate, discipline irrationally, lose his temper or show any signs of fear toward pack members or outsiders. Proper leadership instills confidence into the pack, rewards initiative and operates in a consistent, predictable manner. If the Alpha male were skittish, temperamental and unfair, pack unity would quickly deteriorate, resulting in a diminished level of teamwork. Ultimately, a high mortality rate among the young would follow, threatening the very survival of the species. Responsible leadership involves not only authority, but also knowing how to raise the confidence level of subordinates by acting in a fair and reasonable manner.

The Alpha male wants the other members of the pack to obey him, but he also wants them to become capable and sure of their own abilities. He allowed them to feed first. The young hunters all knew that their leader was very capable and could have fed first had he wanted to. His refusal to do so was interpreted by them not as weakness, but as tribute and praise. Because he was a strong leader and in no way threatened, he could be sure that the young wolves would not interpret his acquiescence as weakness. (Baer and Duno 116-117)

If the leader of the wolf pack was not fair and never allowed the rest of the pack to share in the kill, they would starve to death and there would be no more pack. If the leader randomly attacked pack members, they would lose confidence in him as a leader. If the leader injured his pack when disciplining, he would no longer have a strong healthy pack for hunting. If the pack leader walked around whining and acting stressed all the time, the pack would be stressed and start looking for a stronger leader or try taking control themselves.

Your dog doesn't understand all your actions, but consistent, predictable rules will build confident, capable dogs. If you are in the habit of angry explosions, your dog will be stressed and confused. Dogs understand a quick correction, learn their lesson and get over it. If your dog perceives you as being unfair and unpredictable, he will lose confidence in you as leader and will not feel safe.

Your dog will sense if you're in a constant state of stress or fear causing him to be stressed and insecure. Your fear, anxiety and stress transfer to your dog and a stressed or fearful dog is prone to biting.

A lot of pressure is put on a dog who lacks leadership skills, when placed in a leadership position. It stresses the dog trying to handle situations he is not equipped to manage. Most dogs are happiest and feel a great sense of relief when someone else takes on the leadership role.

To be the best leader for your dog have clear, consistent, predictable rules and boundaries. Be calm and patient when working with your dog, reward desired behaviors and put your dog away if you're frustrated. A good leader provides an enriching, positive environment allowing the dog time to acclimate, develop good social skills, build confidence, develop problem solving capabilities and learn desired behaviors.

Leaders Protect Their Pack

The male grizzly lumbered into the meadow at midday, catching the sleepy wolf pack off-guard. At over nine hundred pounds, he came close to weighing more than all the wolves combined. The bear was either not aware of the pack's presence or else didn't care.

The Alpha male caught the scent of grizzly in his sleep and was on his feet before his eyes were fully open. Guided first by his nose, he quickly caught sight of the bear who was busily digging at some mounded soil about 50 yards to the north, probably looking for grubs or perhaps a marmot in its burrow. Breaking into a full run, the 74-pound timber wolf let out two gruff, percussive sounds that both ended with short, high pitched howl. It was a vocalization he hadn't used all summer. A sound of dire warning, the call to arms was instantly and instinctively understood by all his brethren to mean that their very existence was in peril.

All looked up from their respective resting places to see their leader sprinting toward a monstrous creature that had been, to most of them, only a myth, a feeling. Now it had come upon them and their father was running to meet it without hesitation, almost as if the two were old friends. He ran faster than they had ever seen him run and in a flash the two were together, the bear incredulous at the absurdity of it this small ghostly dog creature appearing from nowhere and flying toward him like a bee driven to madness by the consumption of its hive. The others were at first frozen by the scene, held back by fear and disbelief. After moments that seemed to her like days, the Alpha female flew to the defense of her mate and was quickly followed by the others, all of them, even the five-month-old pups. They had all been instantly changed, raised to a level of solidarity that had never been felt before... (Baer and Duno 98-99)

A dog's instinct to protect his pack is a common reason why strangers get bit by someone's pet dog. A dog who thinks he is in charge will take this job very seriously. Dogs do not always have the ability to judge whether a situation is dangerous or not. Putting a dominate dog in the role of a leader is dangerous, because they likely don't have the capability to exercise good judgment.

An insecure dog may also believe it is his responsibility to protect his family or household if there is no better candidate. Fearful dogs are not capable of handling that responsibility and many times will bite out of fear and uncertainty. Putting a subordinate dog in the role of a leader puts a large amount of stress on that dog and sets them up to fail.

By providing your dog with good leadership, you give them a sense of safety and confidence in your ability to protect them. Their confidence will grow as they gain trust in your capability to maintain control and manage situations. They will begin to let go of fear as their trust and confidence grows. Good leaders are empowering, stable and promote confidence.

As a leader, it is your job to protect your pack by being an advocate for your dog. Learn to interpret your dog's behavior and respect what he is telling you. Know your dog's limits, stay aware of your surroundings and set him up for success. It is your job to stay a step ahead of danger and protect him.

When taking your dog out into a public situation, keep him out of the way of getting bumped into or stepped on. When putting in a down, place under a table or out of the way of traffic. If he's uncomfortable with people approaching, use your body as a barrier to give him space. Watch his behavior for stress or overstimulation. Before he becomes out of control, remove him from the uncomfortable situation. Practice exercises at a distance your dog is easily managed and feels safe. We don't want to put him in a situation where he feels the need to growl or snap.

It can help a dog feel more comfortable in a new environment by communicating with him through previously trained behaviors. Often, dogs are unsure what their responsibility is, so by asking him to sit or down and engage in eye contact, he can be reassured. If your dog is fussy and fidgety, try redirecting with something he knows and see if it helps him settle.

You can use toy play and treats to keep him engaged with you and create a positive association with a new environment. Do not use the treats to force him into a situation he is uncomfortable with.

Do not punish your dog for giving warning signs or growling. Punishing this communication from your dog will create a dog who reacts without warning and will diminish his trust in you. Use this information to do better next time to set him up for success.

Beware of dog parks! It is important to find playmates who are a good match for your dog. We want him to have positive experiences with other dogs. Taking him into a dog park full of dogs with different experiences, agendas and play style can be very overwhelming and develop reactive tendencies. If you see a bully in the park, leave. We have seen many behavior issues develop from dog park interactions. It is your job to keep him safe and that sometimes means walking away when you want to stay. A better option to dog parks is finding people with dogs who play similarly to yours and setting up playdates.

A few signs your dog is stressed:

- Hackles up
- Low growling
- Ears flattened
- Tail tucked
- Tail wags that are quick and low or in between legs
- Tail stiff
- Head turned to side
- Lowered head
- Panting when not hot
- Averting eyes away
- Drooling
- Intense staring
- Closing mouth when was open and relaxed
- Tightening of lips
- Licking nose
- Tongue flicking

- Yawning
- Cowering
- Pancaking
- Stiff body posture
- Seeking places to hide
- Pinning body against yours
- Hiding behind you
- Rolling on back
- Barking and backing away
- Avoidance
- Attempts to flee
- Lunging and nipping
- Pacing

Tips on Protecting Your Dog

- It is ok to say "No" to people asking to pet your dog.
- Keep them out of the way so they do not get stepped on or kicked while in a sit or down.
- Keep their tails out of pathways.
- Use yourself as a barrier if needed.
- Take an air horn or other deterrent when going out for a walk.
- Think ahead how you can set your dog up for success.
- If there is a known aggressive dog in an area, avoid going that way.
- If approaching an out of control dog, try to move off the path or change directions to move away.
- If you are anxious or lack confidence, don't push your dog.
- If you're unsure, say "No."
- Teach an emergency tactical heel position.

Leaders Control Possessions

The two-year-old male wolf walked over to the Alpha male's high spot near the old Jack pine and laid down. The largest wolf in the pack, he outweighed the Alpha by at least l0 pounds and would perhaps one day be his successor. A well-chewed femur bone from an old butt moose lay there. He picked it up in his mouth and began to gnaw on it. The bone had been a favorite of the Alpha ever since the pack brought the Moose down two days before. Now, with the Alpha males' bone, the young male felt comfortable and strong there in his leader's spot that overlooked the entire meadow.

When the young male heard the two young pups coming down the ridge, he knew both Alphas would soon be home. He felt good about that, yet he did not think to get up or even to stop chewing on the bone he had been coveting.

The pups cavorted into the meadow closely followed by their mother, the Alpha female. She toted in, circled the resting pack, then headed over to the high spot where the young male was resting and chewing. She sniffed the scene and gruffed at him several times as if to warn him of his foolishness. He was too enraptured with the bone to respond respectfully to her. She paced nervously and waited.

Just then she caught sight of her mate, who was quietly sitting 20 yards above them on the hill that led to the ridge trail. He was looking down on the scene with calm indifference, as if slightly disappointed and somewhat bored. The young male abruptly stopped his chewing and scented the air, the bone still hanging loosely from his mouth. As he looked above, the Alpha female and her pups quietly left the scene and joined the others below in the meadow. The young male scanned the woods above him and caught sight of his leader calmly staring at him, still in the sitting position, unmoving. Standing now, he dropped the bone and continued to meet the Alpha's gaze. Then the Alpha lowered his head slightly, turning the gaze into a glare. The young male broke eye contact, batted the bone with his big right paw and sauntered over to the meadow to tease one of the juveniles into a game of chase. The Alpha male came down the hill to his spot, lifted his leg on the old Jack pine and lay down, his head resting on the worn femur bone of the old Bull Moose. (Baer and Duno 77-78)

You should be able to safely take anything away from your dog; however, this needs to be taught in a constructive manner. It is very natural for a dog to be possessive; we need to teach him to trust that our presence brings better things.

Our actions often unintentionally add perceived value to a toy, possession or stolen item. Often our first inclination is to chase and scold our dog for taking something we don't want them to have. Canines love the game of possession and by chasing them and losing our patience, we undermine our status in our relationship. A true leader remains calm, acts fairly and does not engage in chasing.

Once a dog has discovered it can keep an item by displaying aggressive behaviors, it can be very difficult to eliminate completely. If your dog growls, snaps or bites when you try to take something away, he is not safe. This is a complicated matter and requires professional help to develop a system of management.

There are too many variables to give written instruction on how to handle possessive aggression issues and if misunderstood someone could get hurt.

A few ways to reduce the risk of inciting aggressive behaviors stemming from possessive tendencies are:

- Absolutely do not chase your dog to retrieve an object, especially if he has stolen the item.
- If your dog steals or picks something up he is not supposed to have, try trading for a treat or another appropriate object.
- Encourage your dog to bring you objects and reward regularly. If it's a dog appropriate object, reward with treat and/or praise and return the object to the dog.

- Sometimes the best way to retrieve an object from your dog is by ignoring him. Your interest places value on the item. Go do something more fun and they will likely leave the object to engage in a more fun game. Return to pick up the item while your dog is elsewhere.
- Teach your dog proper play skills.
- Condition a "Leave It" command to move away from an object for something better.
- A house lead is a very useful tool. You can often pick up the lead and walk him away from the desired object, then pick it up later out of his presence.

Managing your puppy this way will help prevent possessive tendencies. If he is exhibiting aggressive behaviors, get professional help immediately.

Tug play is a game of possession. If you play tug of war with your dog, follow proper toy play etiquette. The game should be played in a constructive manner with a balance of engagement and control. Mouthing, biting or jumping on the owner are not allowed. These behaviors usually indicate over arousal and the game should cease until respectful boundaries are re-established.

Tug-o-war may not be an appropriate game for all dogs, especially if behavior issues already exist. Use extreme caution allowing children to play tug of war with dogs. Most children aren't capable of playing tug in a constructive way and are easily injured by an overzealous dog. Many dogs do not understand children and are less respectful of them.

Children and Leadership

It can be difficult to convince a dog that a child has authority, as it's sometimes hard enough getting him to respect an adult. Adults must step in and help the child gain the respect of the dog. It is not safe for dogs to be dominant over a child because, he may feel the need and he has the right to discipline the child, potentially resulting in a bite. A dominant dog will be inclined to "protect" their children, setting up an environment where a friend could be bitten for innocent play.

Children are physically smaller and have higher pitched voices that can sound like a stress whine to a dog. Children act in strange confusing ways, often play on the floor lower than the dog, have short attention spans and move in funny ways.

It is unfair to expect young children to convince a dog they are in a position of leadership without help. Children have a hard time managing dogs and cannot be expected to maintain control. It is good for children to participate in the feeding, care and training sessions, so the dogs learn to respect and obey them. Children also need to be taught rules on how to engage with dogs.

Help your dog make good decisions by giving him a safe place to escape when feeling tired or overwhelmed. Teach children to leave dogs alone when they are in their safe place. If the dog seems stressed or is trying to control the children's play, send the dog to his "Place."

Rules for children when interacting with dogs:

- Stay away from the dog when he is in his "Place."
- Pet nicely without pulling the hair.
- No pulling on dog's ears, tail or other body parts.
- No climbing or sitting on the dog.
- No chasing the dog, especially to retrieve a stolen object.
- No playing tug-o-war.
- No hitting or kicking the dog.

Rules for parents to keep children and dogs safe:

- Never leave children unsupervised around dogs.
- Do not allow your dog to sleep in children's beds.
- Do not allow strangers to hug your dog.
- Don't let children play tug of war with your dog.
- Don't allow your dog to chase children.
- Don't let your children chase dogs.
- Never allow your dog to jump on children.
- Have your children go out the door before your dog.
- Never allow your dog to put his mouth on children.

Part 4- Constructive Exercises and Games

Play with Your Dog!

By now you may be wondering what to do with your dog? You can and must give your dog positive attention, petting and play time. Physical and mental exercise is critical to having a happy dog. Pent up energy is the root cause of many behavior problems.

You can really enjoy your dog with constructive games such as:

- Retrieving- Not all dogs have a great retrieve instinct, but many do.
- Tricks- Dogs love doing their tricks and earning a treat. They are working animals and get satisfaction out of earning their food.
- Scent Games- Dogs love to use their nose and it is very fun and easy to teach them to find things or people. Kids love playing hide-and-seek with their dog.
- Weight Pulling- If you have a dog who loves to pull, get a comfortable harness and teach him to pull a wagon or something heavy.
- Agility- a common and very wonderful way to enjoy exercising your dog and working together as a team.
- Service Dog Tasks- shutting doors, picking things up for you, turning lights on or off and anything else you can think of that would be handy for your dog to do for you.
- Advanced Obedience- commands at a distance, longer durations, adding distractions, more challenging games.
- Conditioning Exercises- Fun and challenging exercises with physical health benefits.
- Engagement Games- use treats and toys to build a partnership with your dog, improving focus and attitude.

Work and Play

Whether playing, working or hanging out, your dog abides by the same set of rules and is continually learning. Consider how your interactions affect the training of your dog. If you're inconsistent, they will be too.

Most people think of work as hard, boring and unenjoyable and play as fun, exciting, and very enjoyable. Your dog does not perceive work and play as two different things and if taught right will enjoy both equally.

Dogs are aware of who is in charge. They pay attention to who is making and enforcing the rules, regardless of working, playing or relaxing.

People tend to treat their dogs differently when they are working with them versus playing with them. If your dog reacts differently when you are working or playing, it is only because you have changed your behavior, attitude or the rules.

You should make work fun for your dog and play should always have rules.

Work and play are the same to your dog, so use the same set of rules. For example, if you don't want your dog to put its mouth on people, you must never play games with your dog that encourages him to grab your hands or any part of your body or clothes. If you don't want to chase your dog to catch him, then you don't want to play games that encourages him to run from you.

Your dog pays attention to everything you do. They watch you regularly and know your gestures, movements and expressions better than you know yourself. He's learning from you whether you realize it or not.

Dogs do not just learn when you put a leash on them and have a training session; therefore, the way you play and interact with them is critical.

PART 4- CONSTRUCTIVE EXERCISES & GAMES

DO NOT:

- Chase your dog ever, especially if you are trying to retrieve a stolen object from them.
- Allow your dog to have a dominant posture over you.
- Allow your dog to put his mouth on you.
- Allow your dog to jump on you.
- Allow your dog to place his feet on you, unless asked as a trained command.
- Allow your dog to paw at you for attention.
- Play hand or feet games that encourage swinging or biting.
- Swat at their face or stomp with your feet encouraging mouthing or attacking.
- Wrestle with your dog.
- Think, "It is just play so it is okay."
- Play with your dog in destructive ways.

PART 4- CONSTRUCTIVE EXERCISES & GAMES

The Art of Toy Play

We get our dogs to be our companion and friends, so we need to treat our dogs like we would our friends. They're not robots. Dogs have interests and values just like us. Some dogs are driven by food, while others are more into toy play or social interactions. We cannot force our dogs to want or like something just because we think they should.

Observe your dog to learn what is important to him. Interact with him to figure out what he enjoys. Does your dog like to play fetch? Does he like to play tug? Does your dog prefer to be in movement? Is he a heavy chewer? Is food his favorite thing? Is he picky with what he likes for treats? Does he just want to be with you for cuddles and attention? Does he like a combination of the above? Keep these questions in mind as you experiment with the best way to motivate and play with your dog.

There are things you can do to build your dog's drive towards personal play, toys, tug play and food. It's nice to have options when you are trying to teach your dog new behaviors or bring them into new places. Not all dogs will be motivated by all these things. What motivates your dog will depend on his personality and can change situationally.

Make play time fun for both you and your dog. If you're not feeling up to playing or you're unfocused on the session, try again later when you're able to give your full attention to your dog. If we want our dog to be focused on us, rather than distracted by other dogs or smells, we need to give him the same respect. Most of us find it frustrating and rude to be out with a friend who spends the whole time distracted with their phone rather than socializing with you. Don't be that friend to your companion.

Thinking in terms of friendship, consider the way you play with your dog. When playing tug, do you always win and take the toy away? Do you overstimulate him with rough play and get angry when he won't give up the toy? These common mistakes create conflict and reflect negatively on the relationship with your dog. If you always lose at a game, you're likely to quit playing. Games should be challenging enough to be rewarding and fun for both players.

When working to build your relationship through play, you must put forth an effort and challenge him at the level. To build the desire to play tug, allow him win more than he loses, but don't make it too easy. If he loses grip of the toy, tease him a bit by having him chase it rather than shoving it back at him. Structure the game causing him to have a near miss or two before resuming a tug session. The game should be challenging for him, but not so much that he quits. We want to play at a level that inspires him to return with more intensity.

To build on prey drive, the toy should be in motion moving away from the dog. If the toy is still or jumping into the dog's mouth, they're going to be less motivated. Imagine a dog hunting a bunny in the wild. They would chase, catch and shake the prey. The prey would run away trying to escape, not jump in the dog's mouth. Once caught, the prey would struggle, possibly play dead to trick the dog into loosening his grip, then try to escape again. We want to simulate this prey behavior to bring out the dog's natural instinct. A wild animal is not going to lay waiting to be caught or jump in a predator's mouth to be eaten. Keep this idea in mind while you're playing with your dog.

Toy play can be conflicting for some dogs. If we try forcing them to play, they are likely to become resistant. Pushing the toy towards them places a lot of pressure on them and may create avoidance. When we are playing with our dogs from the front, we tend to hover over them, which is very challenging to them and many dogs are intimidated by that type of pressure. Think how you feel interacting with a person who doesn't understand personal space. When you back away, they just keep coming towards you. This is very uncomfortable for most of us. If the dog is not taking the toy, try turning your body to the side and crouching down to be more inviting. Keep the toy in motion moving away from the dog or move it in figure 8's on the floor. If your dog doesn't want to hold the toy while you're holding it, try adding distance by using a flirt pole until they build confidence. Be aware of your body movement that may be causing conflict while you play. Moving towards them, standing over them, over excitement, pushing the toy at them, staring at them and becoming frustrated can all be very intimidating.

PART 4- CONSTRUCTIVE EXERCISES & GAMES

A few rules to tug play:

- Keep play at a rational level by using small movements and a neutral tone.
- Keep dog safe by keeping their spine in alignment and moving toy at the level of the dog.
- Move toy side to side, not up and down.
- Avoid overstimulating play.
- Move toy away from dog in quick, small jerky motions.
- Incorporate control and obedience into play once their confidence is built.
- Avoid conflict in "Outing" by using two toys or treats to teach.
- Avoid conflict in "Outing" by making the toy go dead, waiting for release, then rewarding immediately with more play.
- Offer toy parallel to the ground.
- At the end of play, allow the dog to carry the toy, but don't let them take it to the ground to chew. Keep them moving. If they drop the toy, they lose it. Put them away and go back to retrieve the toy.
- Keep a lead on for better management.
- Steal the toy if the dog loosens grip to chatter up and down toy and make them earn it back.
- Interactions will vary depending on the confidence level and drive of the dog. Adjust accordingly. The same dog may interact differently on a different day.
- Let the dog pull against you rather than thrashing the dog around with extreme movements.
- Let them win a lot but focus on reengagement by moving away while encouraging them to bring it back. Use a lead to prevent them from running off with it to chew.
- Have fun!

Constructive Exercises & Games

Acclimation- Exercises allowing your dog to get comfortable in a new space or environment. Empowers your dog to explore and choose his level of comfort towards stimuli.

Environmental Game- Often, dogs are over stimulated by a new environment or unknown activities going on around them. Allowing your dog to get acclimated will improve your dog's focus on you, resulting in a more effective training session.

1. When entering a new environment allow your dog to sniff, explore, check things out and look around until he begins to settle and looks back at you.
2. As soon as the dog looks at you, reward with personal play, a treat or favorite toy.
3. Interact with him for a minute or less, then release him to check out the surroundings again.
4. Reward with treats or play each time your dog looks back at you.
5. Continue this process until your dog has no interest in wandering and becomes focused on you because your rewards are more interesting than the environment.
6. Work this exercise in all locations until he can handle the stress of a new environment. This exercise builds your dog's trust in you, further helping him to adapt to new environments.
7. If you find your dog is too stimulated for a training session, use this exercise to work up to it. You can resort back to this game at any time. Give him time to adapt before trying the session again.

Exploration Game- Divide his meal into several handful or use treats to place in dishes or boxes and scatter about. Use a long line clipped to the back of their harness and allow them to explore the area to find the food.

Agility- is an obstacle course for dogs and a fun way to exercise and build a working bond between dog and owner. Agility helps insecure dogs gain confidence and can be done for fun or competitively. Competitions are judged on time and accuracy in completing obstacles including jumps, tunnels, A-frames, dog walks, weave poles, teeter totters and a pause table.

AKC Competitive Obedience- AKC Titles can only be earned at trials. Each level of competition, Novice, Open and Utility, require mastering a specific set of skills, with increasing difficulty, before advancing to the next level.

> **Novice (CD)-** class demonstrates good skills in heeling on and off leash, coming, standing for an exam, staying in a sit and down with other dogs.

> **Open (CDX)-** class is mostly off leash and includes retrieving and jumping challenges.

> **Utility (UD)-** class includes scent discrimination, directed retrieves, jumping and silent signal exercises. This is the most difficult class, but higher honors can be achieved.

> **Utility Dog Excellent (UDX)-** achieved by qualifying in Open and Utility classes in the same day.

AKC Family Dog Program- We encourage you to work towards passing CGC, CGCA and CGCU tests and obtaining AKC Tricks Dog titles to focus on your commitment to responsible dog ownership. Titles can be added to your dog's registration.

With the exception of the CGC, dogs will need to be AKC registered, have a PAL or Canine Partners number, that is easily obtained through AKC for any purebred or mixed breed. Find information on titles and registering your dog at www.akc.org.

We offer testing and can assist in preparation through private lessons and frequently practice skills in group classes.

> **AKC Canine Good Citizen (CGC)-** A 10 step test promoting

responsible pet ownership and basic good manners for dogs. Open to all dogs old enough to have completed necessary vaccinations. Test items include greeting a stranger with and without a dog, handling and grooming, sit, down, recall, leash skills and supervised separation.

AKC Community Canine (CGCA)- A 10 step test to evaluate the dog's skills in a natural setting. Must have a CGC title on record.

Urban CGC (CGCU)- A 10 step public access test to demonstrate well-mannered, well-trained skills in an urban setting. Must have a CGC title on record.

AKC Tricks Titles- Fun way to show off your dog's talents and add titles to their resume. We offer testing for Novice Trick Dog (TKN), Intermediate Trick Dog (TKI), Advanced Trick Dog (TKA) and Performer Trick Dog (TKP) titles.

Back Packing- Hiking with your dog can be enjoyable with proper care. Make sure your dog is healthy and structurally sound to carry a pack. Build up endurance for longer distances and tougher terrain as you would yourself. Pay attention to their energy level, if lagging they're likely reaching their limit.

Check your dog's pads for cuts, back for soreness and coat for grass seeds during and after hikes. Your dog may be able to carry a small pack of his own but keep it under 10% of their body weight and only if they are fit and healthy. Start with very little weight and build up.

Box Game- Game using a cardboard box that promotes cognitive thinking by encouraging them to offer behaviors for rewards. This exercise works to teach the dog body awareness, to use each foot separately and helps build confidence. Once proficient, the box can be used to communicate other desired behaviors by placing it in or on a location where you would like him to go.

Use a shallow, appropriately sized cardboard box, treats and clicker if applicable.

1. Without using words, get your dog interested in the box by tossing treats in it. Once he puts a foot in the box, reward with click or positive word like "Yes" or "Good," while continuing to toss treats into the box.
2. Give your release and throw a cookie outside the box.
3. Reset him and repeat tossing cookies into the box until he has stepped in several times.
4. Once your dog knows the box isn't weird and he is willingly stepping in, stop dropping treats into the box and let him think about what got him the reward.
5. As soon as a foot touches the box mark with "Yes," "Good" or click and treat. You may need to start by rewarding for looking at the box.
6. Release and repeat several times.
7. Once your dog fully understands placing one foot in the box, wait for him to put two feet in the box.
8. Say "Yes," "Good" or click, reward and release each time he is successful.
9. Continue until he gets all four feet in the box.
10. Wait for him to remain in the box for a little longer.
11. Work your dog to only have the back feet in or to back up into the box.
12. Continuously change your position, so he learns to adjust and move his body.
13. Add distance to the box game.
14. You can change the box for a stool, bin or hoop.
15. Once your dog is doing well with other items like a stool, ask him to put front feet up and step to the side using their back feet. Do this in both directions.
16. Continue this exercise using less pressure and decreased movement from you. Try only giving some direction.
17. Now try putting the back feet up while moving their front feet around the object in both directions.

PART 4- CONSTRUCTIVE EXERCISES & GAMES

Calming Exercises- are good to teach the dogs how to calm down or settle quickly.

Lying on Side- Work on teaching the dog to lie down on its side in a calm, comfortable environment. Often, they are calmer in this position.

1. Have the dog lay down.
2. Start turning his head towards his shoulder and his body should start to roll on its side.
3. Reward with soft petting, cookies and soft talking.
4. You may need to achieve this in stages by rewarding for moving head to shoulder, as he starts to roll to his side, as he rolls onto his side and for holding the position.
5. Once you can get him onto his side easily, work to have him hold the position. Pet with long strokes and light pressure from the back of his head to tail or give gentle massage to help calm him.
6. Once he is calm and enjoying the attention, release him to get up.
7. After releasing, you can play tug or use personal play as a reward.
8. You can then repeat the calming process to teach him how to go from a state of arousal to calm.
9. Once he settles easily in a calm environment, add distractions while working the exercise.
10. Once he can handle a variety of distractions in a known environment, work the exercise in new environments. Working this exercise in many environments will broaden their calm demeanor in all situations.

Eye Contact with Distractions- Objective is to teach your dog to maintain eye contact with you while distractions occur.

1. Start the training by holding a treat or toy to one side of your dog's head and reward when he looks at you and ignores the treat or toy.
2. When he understands the previous step, hold a toy or treat on both sides of his head until he maintains eye contact, mark and reward.

3. Add movement to your hands while holding a treat or toy, mark and reward when he maintains eye contact.
4. Increase your movement by lowering and raising your arms.
5. Add another distraction like a person in the room while maintaining eye contact.
6. Have another person hold an exciting object while the dog maintains eye contact with you. This also reinforces self-control.
7. Practice in new environments, always marking and rewarding success.

Calm to Play- Good for working on moving from play mode to a calm mode, teaching self-control and proper play skills.

1. Play with your dog on your knees with his favorite toy, then steal the toy from your dog and quickly hide it between your legs. You may need to make the toy boring or use a release word if trained to get the toy.
2. Allow your dog to bark, scratch and try to get it.
3. When the dog calms down on his own, by lying down or sitting, tell him "Good" and release him to play with the toy again.
   Note: This will take time and patience for the dog and owner to work through in the beginning, but the dog will learn the quicker he calms down, the faster he can play again.
4. Do not give your dog any direction as to what you want him to do, let him figure it out by offering behaviors.
5. You can do this game on a leash to make sure he doesn't wonder off.
6. Reassure your dog when he is offering behaviors and performing correctly.

Cart Pulling- Pulling a cart or sled can be a fun way to exercise your dog. Your dog must be physically fit, healthy and proper training must precede.

Catch Games- Catching a Frisbee, ball or popcorn can be a joyous game. Dogs don't know how to catch naturally; it is a learned behavior. Once they've learned the concept of opening their mouth to receive an object, practice will refine the skill. Do not throw any hard objects or anything

that may cause injury to their teeth or mouth. Make sure any thrown object is big enough they can't accidently swallow it. Take care not to throw objects too high causing the dog to twist and land oddly.
Start by teasing your dog with an object like a Frisbee or soft rope. Drop into his opened mouth and praise for a good catch. Proceed to short tosses after building excitement for the object. Be patient, it may take some time. If he is confident enough to try, he'll get it. Tossing treats can be a great incentive for them to try to catch something. Once the concept is achieved, practice with his favorite toy or treats to hone in the skill. Maintain control of the game by using a long line, treats or other rewards to have him return the object.

Cavalettis- Place multiple boards on the ground or very low jumps equal distances apart. Start by measuring your dog's height from floor to withers and placing the cavalettis that distance apart. Get him comfortable walking through them slowly without knocking them. Once they are good at walking you can try trotting. You can add difficulty by having him change direction in the middle of the cavalettis. Once he has good awareness of his feet placement, you can have variable distances or messy cavalettis.

Coming Steps and Games- Developing a reliable come is a process that takes several weeks and is best trained as a positively conditioned response. Spending time building a fun, engaging relationship with your dog will help a lot in the training process. Coming to you must always be rewarded with something your dog considers high value.
Never reprimand your dog for coming to you, even if you are frustrated by his behavior. If he tries to engage you in catch me games, use your leash to manage him and ask for an alternative behavior. Grabbing at him will escalate this behavior. We want to teach him that coming to us brings good things, as do our hands reaching towards him.

Coming involves several training components. A desired come includes coming to you from any distance away from any distractions. Upon reaching you, he should sit in front of you, facing you with eye contact and should remain in place until released. To develop a good come, each component needs to be taught and practice individually before putting it all together. When putting the pieces together mark and reward at various steps of the process. Some dogs will come and sit easily, others may need to be rewarded for getting to you, then asked to sit in front and rewarded again. Once your dog is sitting in front of you, work on eye contact while holding his position and not wandering off until you give the release. Once he understands all the components of the come, make rewards variable by rewarding at varying steps of the process. Always reward!

Remember to always stay positive and set your dog up for success. Always praise and reward your dog for coming. You do not have to wait until your dog gets to you to praise, start verbal encouragement from the moment he first responds to you calling. This will make you more exciting and increase your chances that he come all the way to you. You can apply quick pressure to the lead to get his attention. Take in the excess line as he approaches so you can prevent him from wandering off if he gets distracted along the way. Keep your attitude, tone and posture positive. Make it fun and keep tasty treats and/or toys handy!!! Reward every time he comes to you.

1. Have a stash of high value treats handy so while going about your day, you can call your dog and give a treat. Randomly throughout the day call him and reward with a treat and praise when he comes to you. Do this in different rooms of the house and while you are doing a variety of activities. Treat him, tell him how smart he is and let him go back to what he was doing.
2. To begin a more formal recall, start with your dog on a six foot lead in an area with minimal distractions. Back away while calling him enthusiastically. Reward with treats and praise when he gets to you.
3. Let him get distracted and call him to you. Back up if he gets distracted or stops short, to draw him closer to you.
4. Once he is coming reliably, ask for a sit when he gets to you.
5. Once he is coming and sitting reliably, add eye contact.
6. Practice having him come, sit and hold eye contact until you release him. Reward variably throughout the process.
7. Practice the coming components in a new low distraction

environment.

8. Begin generalizing coming on a short lead into several new environments with different low-level distractions.
9. Add a new distraction such as a friend, toy, food or another dog in a familiar, secure environment and practice calling him using a short lead.
10. Repeat the steps above using a 15' – 25' long line.
11. Increase the level of distractions as he improves, setting him up to succeed.
12. Practice in as many locations that you can.
13. In a secure area practice coming by dropping the long line and allowing him to drag it. Call him and start praising when he first responds. Cheer him on all the way to you and reward.

> **TIP:** If he gets distracted and doesn't come, calmly walk towards the end of lead and pick it up. Reel in the excess lead, call your dog again, applying quick tension and run back until you get his attention and he comes to you. Reward him when he gets to you.

14. Work your dog in secure areas using a long line to continue increasing the distance you call your dog from.
15. Generalize the training to new locations by starting with a short lead and increasing the distance with the use of a long line.
16. Continue adding new distractions to call him past or away from.
17. Make coming fun by playing the coming game with a friend or other games described below. Games can be incorporated during any phase of the process.
18. Reward every time! Remember: Reinforcement drives behavior. If you want a reliable come, you are going to have to pay top dollar for it.

See the following chart for a sample of how you might progress as you teach your dog a reliable come.

STEPS TO A RELIABLE COME

Inside house with house lead, runbacks

Quiet , secure backyard with house lead, runbacks

Up steps with short lead

From another room in the house

Run backs outside, low distraction

Short lead, outside, from low distraction

Long line, outside, from low distraction

Medium distraction, | short lead, runbacks, parking Lot

High distraction, | short lead, runbacks, park

Low distraction, backyard, | long line, outdoors

Medium distraction, low use park, | long line, outdoors

High distraction, busy park, | long line, outdoors

Outdoor, low distraction, secure yard, | dropped long line

Long distance, low distraction, secure, | dropped line

Outdoors, secure, medium distraction, park, | dropped line

Outdoor, secure, high distraction, dropped line

Off-leash, secure, low, medium then high distraction

Adding Distractions and Generalizing-

Sounds- vehicle noises, people talking, dogs barking, doors opening and closing, knocking, doorbells, household noises, etc.

Locations- parking lots, parks, trail heads, ball fields, friend's house, boat launch, anywhere you go.

Surfaces- stairs, grass, woods, pavement, water, board walk, etc.

Objects- food, toys, people, animals, cars, new sights, etc.

Activities- people playing frisbee, walking dogs, riding bikes, pushing strollers, running, throwing a ball, etc.

Come Through Legs- Works the same as Toss and Move, except have your dog run between your legs each time to get the treat. Toss the treat back between your legs with dog in front of you and say, "Get It." You will need to start him close enough to lure through your legs until he understands the game. While he goes for the treat, move away, turn towards him, call him to come and as he approaches, toss the treat between your legs saying, "Get It." Repeat process several times making it fun, fast-paced and rewarding. This exercise helps build their excitement to come straight back to you quickly.

Family Come Fun- This game reinforces coming in a fun, engaging way the whole family can play. It can be played with two or more players. This is a positive only game; corrections are not allowed. Attach a 20'-30' long line to your dog to keep him safe. The long line is a tool used to set your dog up for success. It can be used to prevent the dog from wandering off or assist in completing the task without force or a correction. It can be reeled in as they approach to prevent detouring to a distraction. You can move down the line to decrease distance to your dog while maintaining a neutral composure. Use your voice, enthusiasm, baiting and movement to encourage the behaviors you want. We want 100% success. If playing in an unsecure area, have one person hold the line, taking care not to unintentionally correct the dog.

Make sure each player has a pocket full of high value treats and spread out 20'-30' apart. Call your dog back and forth with a high level of enthusiasm and high value rewards at each stop. Keep the game moving quickly and make it fun. Only one person calls the dog at a time. If more than two people are playing, change the pattern to keep it interesting. Stop the game while your dog is still engaged and enjoying it.

Restrained Come- Have someone your dog is comfortable with hold him by his chest or a lead clipped to the back of a harness. Show your dog you have treats or his favorite toy and walk away. Turn, crouch down and call him to you while he is still restrained. Allow him to push into the hands of the helper or harness before releasing him to come to you. Reward with treats or play and lots of enthusiasm as soon as he gets to you. You can use a long line thread through a back tie to work this alone.

Runbacks- Facing your dog, back up drawing them into the front position (sitting in front of you and facing you with eye contact). Once in front position, take a few steps back and reward for moving with you, repeatedly, to focus on the coming to front piece of the come. Be sure to reward each time to build a strong positive association.

While out for a walk, you can incorporate runbacks to continue building a conditioned response to come. As you're walking, start backing up and call to front. Reward and resume walk. Do this randomly throughout your walks.

Use runbacks when your dog gets distracted on his way to you. Do not reward for disengaging, rather regain your dog's attention by backing up a few steps and drawing him in. You may need to take ahold of the leash or shorten your grip to prevent him from wandering off further. Reward when comes to front and gives eye contact.

Use rapid fire runbacks for a dog who blows you off once he gets to you to work on coming to front, sitting and engaging with eye contact. Rapid fire in this context means take a step or two back while your dog moves with you and sits when you stop. Do this quickly and repeatedly, rewarding each time. Only reward for being engaged.

Toss and Move- Dogs are drawn towards things moving away from them. Establish a word that allows your dog to go get a treat or toy, such as "Get It." Toss a treat away from you, tell your dog "Get It," and while they go to the treat move in the opposite direction. When they look, toss the treat away from the dog past your body and say, "Get It." While he gets the treat run back to the starting point. When he looks, toss a treat away from him past your body and repeat the process several times, making it fun, fast-paced and rewarding.

Conditioned Relaxation Response (Parking the Dog)- Start in a quiet area with minimal distractions. Sit with your foot on the leash slightly shorter than height of your dog. Sit calmly until he lies down and remains calm. You do not need to give a command; this exercise is intended to teach the dog to exhibit calm behavior and relax when you sit. Slowly increase the amount of time spent in a calm, down position.

Conditioning Exercises- There are a variety of exercises that are excellent for the physical fitness of your dog and also work to build trust, engagement, confidence, body awareness and joy. Incorporating exercises using balance discs, wobble boards, rocker boards, cavaletti's, platforms, weaves and other balancing equipment has a multitude of benefits.

Cone Game- Teaching the dog to go around a cone or other objects in both directions. The cone game teaches the dog to look for an obstacle. You can use many types of objects to work this game, like posts, trees, light poles and fire hydrants. If you do agility, this exercise is good for teaching your dog to look for obstacles to offer, as well as learn to go around jumps.

Strategy 1: Start teaching the cone game by walking up next to the cone with your dog on the opposite side of your body. Once he takes a step

PART 4- CONSTRUCTIVE EXERCISES & GAMES

towards the cone, mark and toss the treat around and past the cone.
To have him go right, place your dog on your left and approach the cone
standing to its left. Wait for him to step to the right, mark with "Good,"
draw him around the cone by tossing the treat behind you to the right.

To have him go left, approach the cone with your dog on your right, stand
to the right of the cone, wait for him to step to the left, mark and reward
with a treat tossed behind you to the left.

As he understands moving around the cone, slowly move back to increase
the distance.
If your dog wanders off in the wrong direction, reset by walking away and
re-approaching the cone.

Strategy 2: Toss treats strategically around the cone to get your dog
moving around it. I start this exercise on my knees then work to my feet
once they start understanding the concept of going around the cone.
There is no need for words, this game is designed to motivate them to
figure out the desired behavior and offer it.

1. Start by strategically dropping cookies around the cone working
   the dog in a circle around it.
2. Have him pass between you and the cone to go around it.
3. Change the direction and coax him to circle the other way.
4. As the dog starts going around the cone easily, quit coaxing him
   around it. Mark and reward any movement towards the cone.
5. Toss the treat to a good starting point to set him up to try again.
6. As he learns to move towards the cone wait for him to get a
   quarter of the way around the cone before marking and
   rewarding to set up for next rep.
7. Once he is reliable at a quarter turn, advance to a half turn.
8. As he comes around the cone, mark and reward by tossing a treat,
   complete the circle and setting him up for the next rep.
9. Continue advancing him until he reliably circles the entire cone
   including passing in between you and the cone.
10. Remember to practice in both directions.

11. Once your dog is going around the cone completely in both directions, hold out for two evolutions around the cone.
12. Slowly start increasing the distance between you and the cone, so your dog begins moving away from you to go around the cone.
13. Start playing this game at parks and other locations by having him go around poles, trees or other imaginative objects. Generalizing will broaden their understanding and desire to offer behaviors that have paid in the past.

Crate Game- A method to make crating a positive experience. See steps for Crate Training in Part 2- Developing Household and Social Skills.

Engagement Games- Games to promote positive interactions and focus between you and your dog.

Check-In's- While walking your dog on a loose leash, watch for any eye contact or checking in. Reward with "Good" and give a treat each time he checks in. You can also reward with toy play each time he looks at you. Use body movements, turns and an upbeat voice to encourage the checking-in behavior. You can use a treat in your hand to draw a quick line from their nose to your eyes that will often get his attention when first starting. Eliminate the extra help and luring once he gets the idea, wait for him to offer the behavior, capture and reward. Slowly increase amount of time before rewarding.

Eye Contact- Once your dog understands offering eye contact, work to increase the duration. Mix-up duration with rewarding for easy wins. Duration work should be variable versus steady increases. Time how long you can keep your dog's focus on you using treats, toys and verbal reinforcement. No touching or restraining. For added difficulty, add distractions such as someone dropping food or bouncing a ball. Practice in various locations.

Flirt Pole- A pole with a toy attached to a rope on the end. Use for building prey drive and a fun way for indoor exercise. They are great for use with insecure dogs because it removes body pressure. Use the pole to jerk the toy in a motion away from your dog. If your dog goes after it, quickly jerk away again. If he catches it use little flicks of the toy to keep him engaged. If he drops it, jerk it away again, letting him chase and catch it alternatingly.

GRC Dogsports- *Gameness, Relationship and Control Dogsports* is a new dog sport with competitions in social responsibility, spring pole, wall climb, weight pull and slat mill races. The focus of GRC is to train dogs who thrive in our world and provide a healthy place to orient their natural drive. See grcdogsports.com for more information. A local club is in the process of development. Join the Facebook group, *A Canine Experience Events and Chats* for updates.

Front- Asking your dog to come to the front of your body, sit and face you. Use treats to draw your dog close to your body. Practice having him move with you while remaining directly in front of you. Step back and turn right and left while he maintains his position directly in front of you, adjusting himself as needed. The front position with a step back and a right and left turn is part of the GRC Social Responsibility test.

Herding- Can be applied to practical application or sport. Herding is the act of bringing individual animals together and moving them from place to place in a group. Many farmers and ranchers use herding dogs to maintain their herds.

IPO- Formerly known as Schutzhund is a three-part sport including tracking, obedience and protection.

Leash Walking- (Notes from *Puppy Culture* DVD Series)

> Start practicing walking off-leash in safely fenced area, puppies follow anything that move. Start walking, click and treat anytime they get near your left side. Let the puppy work it out. Once the puppy understands treats comes from being by you, start adding two steps, three steps......working up to more steps. Once walking several steps with you, start walking in small circles positioning the puppy on the inside. Once he/she understands following,

change one thing at a time by adding a collar, then a leash. If shaped correctly, the puppy should automatically follow when called and you start walking.

The leash is not a training tool, it is a backup like a climber's safety rope. When the puppy hits the end of the leash, it activates an opposition reflex and he will naturally fight against it. Let the leash out and keep moving forward. Mark and reward when the puppy starts moving back toward you. Avoid tugging on the leash. He will begin to learn to move toward you when feeling the lead tighten. Increase the difficulty by adding more steps a few at a time. Give him a break after a short session, so the puppy has time to process what he's learned.

Short sessions with rest in between is very powerful at a young age. Longer distances and fewer treats will come in time. We are often asked when it is the right time to wean the puppy off food in exchange for a behavior. Why be in such a hurry to not give a dog treats? Thin the ratio...sure, but a relationship is a history of reinforcement. The goal should be to find as many opportunities as possible to give a dog a treat. That will build a relationship.

Human entitlement leads people to the idea that dogs should respond to a command and they should just be obedient. People feel they have been let down if they must pay for a behavior. The reality is, behavior is a tool animals use to manipulate their environment that consequently helps them to survive in the world. We can capitalize on this or ignore it at our own peril. It is a myth to think they should just do it. (Killion et.al.)

Leave It Exercises- Used to teach your dog to turn away from an object or distraction; it is not pulling him away.

    Food Drop- Drop a treat in front of your dog while restraining so he cannot get to it, say "Leave It" and lure him away using another treat. Move away from the dropped treat as much as needed to redirect dog's attention to the treat in your hand. Reinforce with "Good" and give the treat from your hand. Repeat until your dog starts looking at you without luring. Once he understands "Leave It" with dropped food, you can practice applying to other distractions. Do not use the leash to pull your dog away, we want him to turn and move away on his own.

Enticement Row

1. Place row of enticing objects- bones, toys, chews, bag of treats etc. to walk your dog past.
2. Use a high value treat to lure dog away from the object immediately after saying "Leave It." Give yourself space and turn away from the object with your body while luring your dog.
3. Take several steps with your dog on the outside of your body rather than trying to move into your dog.
4. Move away until he disengages from the object.
5. Repeat until he responds without luring him.
6. Once he turns away without a lure, solicit eye contact and then reward.
7. Work to include eye contact as an automatic response after turning away from an object when asked to "Leave It."
8. To increase difficulty, weave through objects.
9. Generalize with a variety of distractions and enticing objects.

Toy Toss- Place your dog on pause table, bed or down stay next to a table with dog toys. Toss toys into a laundry basket while your dog stays in place. Also practice while he remains in a sit and a down.

Obstacles- Obstacles can be created using your imagination and random items around the house. Ladders, wire spools, dog ramps, boards, bricks, wagons, chairs and other random objects can be used to create fun obstacles for your dog to manipulate. Secure as needed to and avoid anything with protruding parts or sharp edges. Do not force your dog onto obstacles. Allow them to experiment and advance as they feel comfortable. Be prepared to spot them in case they loose balance or misstep. A good harness will help with spotting. Practice spotting when it is not needed so your dog gets comfortable with you assisting him and you build in some muscle memory for when you're needed.

Paper Plate Races- A fun way to work on going out to a target and coming back to a sit in front of you. Races are run in pairs, but practice can be done individually. Have your dog sit and wait while you place a treat on a paper plate a few steps away. Return to your dog and tell him to "Get It." Once he reaches the plate, call him to you as quickly as possible and get him to sit in front of you. Increase the distance until you reach at least 60', the formal distance of the *Dick Russell Paper Plate Race*.

Retrieving- Maintain control by using a long line. Teach your dog to return with the toy and give on command. If he is resistant to giving you the toy or hasn't been taught "Out," use a second toy to begin teaching the "Out." Avoid creating conflict in recovering the toy by exchanging for another toy or treat to develop a positive association with giving you the toy.

You can add teaching your dog to sit and wait while you throw the toy, then send him to retrieve it on command. Use a long line, two of your dog's favorite toys, treats and a positive tone to teach your dog how to play the game. Teach the components of the retrieve separately: coming, picking up the toy, holding the toy, movement with the toy, going out to the toy, giving you the toy, and sitting and waiting can all be taught individually then chained together. Shaping is a very effective means of training the individual components of the retrieve, then chaining the behaviors together.

Some dogs play the game naturally and will just need to be taught the rules others will need a more structured approach. If a dog has no interest in retrieving, it is very difficult to teach.

> *TIP 1: Do not chase your dog to retrieve the item from him. If he does not return, move down the long line to decrease the distance to your dog and use the other toy to get him re-engaged.*

TIP 2: Do not worry if he drops the toy as he returns, reward him for coming to you. If he frequently returns without the toy, make very short throws and reward him for carrying the toy a step or two. Continue lengthening the distance of the retrieve as he becomes successful at shorter distances.

Searching for Objects- Training your dog to find a specific object is a fun game for you and your dog. They can be taught to indicate the location of the object and/or bring it to you. The options are endless from teaching to find their own toys, your cell phone or keys, or to more serious objects like drugs, explosives or mold.

There are many ways to teach this skill. I've included one simple process using scent pans in the Appendix under "Using Scent Pans to Teach Your Dog to Find an Object."

Searching for People or Pets- You can teach your dog to find a specific person or pet, people in general or varying people or animals.

You will need two people for this game, a hider and a handler. You can play the game inside or outside. Use a buckle collar or harness and a long line for better control.

To start, have one person hold your dog while the other hides in an easy place. Let your dog see the person leave, it is OK if he pulls on the leash and wants to follow. The person leaving can get the dogs attention with a treat or toy as they leave to hide. The hider running away will help excite your dog and create the desire to chase. As soon as the person is out of sight, let your dog move towards the hider. It is OK if he pulls, you want him to lead you to the person. Once your dog finds the person, have a party with treats and/or toys. As he understands the game, increase the distance to the hider.

Add a command to search such as "Search" or "Find." Make sure they have a successful find every time to build their confidence in the game.

Once he understands the game, have someone hide in a very simple location without your dog seeing the hider leave. Once he learns the game can be played without seeing the person hide, slowly increase the difficulty. Larger areas, more time lapse between the person hiding and your dog beginning the search, difficult terrain, hard surfaces like pavement, hot days, snow coverage and crazy wind are all examples of increased difficulty.

A recall/re-find can be implemented, which means they find the person, return to you, indicate and take you to the person. Play the coming game between handler and hider to create this pattern. Cue the indicator into the re-find when the dog returns to the handler, after finding the hider. The indicator will have to be taught separately and can be a bark, spin, tug or other fluid action.

Slat Mill- A dog-propelled treadmill used for exercise and building speed and endurance. *GRC Dogsports* offers a Slat Mill Racing competition.

Spring Pole- A free hanging tug toy used to work on drive control without engaging in bite work or the need of a decoy. *GRC Dogsports* offers a competition involving controlling a dog from a distance incorporating various obedience commands including when to tug and release the toy.

Spotting- Safety when working your dog on obstacles is very important. Spotting is a way to assist your dog if he over or under jumps and to minimize the impact of jumping off or over high objects.

Spotting is NOT catching your dog as he is free falling through the air. If this happens, something went wrong. Spotting is being ready to help your dog in the moment something goes wrong, so it is barely apparent.

A well fitted harness should be used when participating in urban agility and other activities where spotting may be necessary. The harness should have wide straps with a V-neck that sits across the sternum and goes between the front legs allowing the shoulders to move freely. A rear strap should span across the ribcage, not the abdomen, behind the armpits. There should be a leash attachment on the back over the center of gravity. We do not want them tipping forward or back when spotting. Attach your leash to the back of the harness. Hold the leash so it comes up from the back and there is very little slack. Manage any excess leash so it does not get wrapped up or interfere with your dog's movement in anyway. Keep the leash out of your dog's way and be prepared to use it to offer assistance when your dog needs it.

If your dog overjumps onto an obstacle, use your hand on his chest to slow him down and prevent him from falling off the other side. Move into a spotting position after he jumps so you do not get in their way.

If he under jumps you have two options: help him onto the object or help him to the ground. Which depends on what your dog wants to do, support his momentum. Give him a little boost to help him onto the object or use your leash to help with a soft landing back to the ground.

To help reduce the impact from jumping off a high obstacle, use your leash clipped to the back of the harness, shortened and taught, to apply upward pressure to soften the blow as your dog jumps down. You can also help him down by placing your hand under his ribcage and lifting him down or teaching him to put his front feet on you so you can lower him down.

Teach him to stand while you reach under his rib cage and lift from a low obstacle so he gets use to the feeling and doesn't fight the help. Also teach him to put his front feet on you and to be lowered. Practice spotting in a controlled setting before it needs to be applied.

The shoulder height rule gives some guidelines to when spotting should be incorporated. If jumping onto a hard surface, max height without spotting should be shoulder height. If jumping onto a soft surface, up to 2X shoulder height should be the maximum without spotting. This should be modified for dogs who are overweight, out of shape, aged or under 18 months. Puppies under 18 months should be limited to stopper pad height until six-months, then add 1" per month until their growth plates are closed (about 18 months). Consider the accumulative stress and amount of impact being absorbed when determining how much assistance your dog needs.

All your spotting skills should be practiced before they are needed so you have good muscle memory and your dog gets use to your assistance. You can use a second person to also help with spotting. Your dog should be comfortable with any helper you use handling him.

Targeting- Teaching to go to a target can be very helpful in distance and directional work where the dog is moving away from the handler. Targets are commonly used in agility to teach contact points.

> **Send out Game-** Hold your dog by the collar while he watches as you place a treat in a bowl. Move him away from the bowl a few feet. When he is looking at the bowl, release him to go to it. Praise and repeat multiple times. Add a cue like "Get It" when you release him to the bowl. Slowly increase the distance to the bowl. Once he understands the game, have him sit next to you and wait until you release him with the cue to go "Get It." Work on increasing the distance to the target and the control to only go when sent.

> **Foot Target-** Let your dog watch you place a non-slip target on the floor a couple feet in front of you. When he looks at the target, mark and reward by tossing the treat a couple feet away. If he loses interest, pick up the target and set it back down. Mark and reward every time he looks at the target by tossing a treat. Once he understands looking at the target earns a reward, wait for him to make a motion towards it, mark and reward until he reliably motions towards it. Wait for a step towards the target, mark and reward until he reliably steps towards it. Mark and reward as he gets closer to the target working to get him to touch it with a foot. Continue working to have him reliably go to the target, touch it with a foot and return for a treat. Once he understands this from a couple feet away, increase the distance to the target. Toss the treat behind you when rewarding to build his drive to return to you quickly.

PART 4- CONSTRUCTIVE EXERCISES & GAMES

Touch- Teaching your dog to touch your hand or a touch stick can be used to train other behaviors. You can teach them to follow your hand or stick to lure into positions, guide to a location or move in a specific direction. A hand touch is also commonly used to redirect a dog in a stimulating environment, often taught as an emergency come.

It is generally pretty easy to teach a touch to hand because they are used to coming to your hand for a treat. Hold out your flat hand at his eye level. When your dog comes to investigate your hand say "Good" and reward him. Do this repeatedly until he understands touching your hand earns a reward. Make it harder by moving your hand to different levels, eventually moving high enough he needs to pop up to touch it. Incorporate coming to your hand from more distance and from different directions. Once he's really good at touching your hand when you present it, practice in locations with distractions.

Tracking/Trailing- Tracking dogs follow the trail of a person or animal. The dog is generally taken to the person or animal's last known place. They are either trained to start on a hot trail or presented with an article containing the scent of who they are to locate. Once they pick up the scent of the subject, they follow the trail to the person or animal. The dog is worked on a longline and takes the handler directly to the person or animal to be found.

Start by having someone scuff their feet on the ground a few feet and place a target (lid or scent pad with a treat). Have the dog sniff the start point and follow to the target. Slowly extend the distance of the trail, using targets at the turns. Scent pads can be used along the trail for variable or strategic reinforcement. When they reliably follow a fresh trail, let the trail age, slowly extending the aging period.

Tricks- Tricks are fun to teach and show off. Have fun with the lessons and use luring, markers and treats to teach your dog the desired behavior. Lure by keeping a treat close to your dog's nose, inside your hand so he can't grab it. Another option is to first teach him to follow a touch stick, then use the stick to lure. Have your dog follow the lure into desired position or direction you want him to move. You may need to give a little help with your hands or leash to direct him. Do not force, just give him gentle guidance if needed.

Shaping using a clicker is great way to teach new tricks. Break the desired behavior down into incremental movements, mark and reward each step until the behavior is achieved. This may take several sessions. Using a lure to show them the desired behavior can be helpful to start this process but eliminate luring as quickly as possible.

Some fun tricks you can train using lures and/or shaping include spin right, spin left, weave between legs, around (into heel position), left swing heel, over, under, rollover, play dead, sit pretty, back up, leave it with treats nearby or on paws, flip treat from nose and catch, jump (only if over 1 year old), dance, high five, shake, speak, hugs, etc.

Tricks requiring your dog to put their feet on you should be avoided if your dog's showing any signs of aggression or controlling behaviors.

Tricks for Treats-

Luring- When using treats for luring, place the treat between two fingers and lure with an open hand. Another option is to teach your dog to touch your hand as a target, lure with your hand and reward with a treat.

Open & Close- To save your hands, teach your dog to take a treat from your flat hand when you say "Okay." Hold a treat inside your closed hand. Let you dog try to get it from your hand. As soon as he backs away, open your hand, say "Okay" and allow him to get the treat.

Once he understands to back away from your closed hand to earn the treat, open your hand. When your dog comes for the treat, close your hand quickly. When he backs away, open your hand and say "Okay" to allow him the treat. Repeat until he understands to only take the treat when you say "Okay."

Practice increasing the amount of time before he receives the treat. Build his reliability by moving your open hand with the treat closer to him, near his mouth, under his chin and closing your hand quickly if he goes for it. Always say "Okay" and offer the treat with an open hand to allow him to take it.

Target- You can put a treat on a target to work on sending your dog away or to a specific place. A target could be a bowl, paper plate, FitPAW target, yogurt lid or any variety of objects.

Treat Dispenser- A remote controlled device that drops treats at the push of a button. Great for crate training, targeting, building confidence, rewarding at a distance or a specific location.

Treat Toss- Rather than delivering a treat from your hand you can toss the treat strategically to set your dog up for the next exercise. This is a great way to accomplish several repetitions in a short period of time, really solidifying a behavior.

Tactical Heel (Middle/In-Line)- Positioning your dog between your legs and teaching them to move with you while in that position is a great emergency tactic. You can keep your dog safe while in this position. Teaching him to come into this position from wherever he is at is highly recommended. Tactical heeling with a step forward, back and a right and left turn is a component of the GRC Social Responsibility test.

Tugging- Tug games are fun for many dogs and owners, can build confidence and be used as a reward. Clear boundaries need to be established around the game of tug. Your dog should never put his mouth on you and overstimulation needs to be avoided. Tug play is not safe with all dogs. See "Work and Play" and "The Art of Toy Play" at the beginning of Part 4- Constructive Exercises and Games for tips on tugging.

Urban Agility/Parkour- Urban agility is a great way to get more out of your walks. Incorporate the objects in the environment as obstacles to place two or four feet on, revolve around, go around, weave, jump, straddle, side-step, go through, go under, go over, get in, balance on, etc.

PART 4- CONSTRUCTIVE EXERCISES & GAMES

Have fun with it. You will find your dog stays more engaged when you are interacting rather than just walking. You can earn Parkour titles by submitting videos to *International Dog Parkour Association*. You can find information on titles, rules and resources at https://www.dogparkour.org/home.

Waiting and Stay Exercises-

Proofing Stays- Add distractions while dog remains in stay. Ideas of distractions:
- hopping on one foot
- waving your arms around
- turn away from the dog
- Kids/strangers walking by
- Kids/strangers running by
- Kids/strangers run by yelling and waving arms
- Another dog walks by
- Owner interacting with another dog
- Rolling/bouncing a ball
- Stand on a chair
- Eat food while sitting in a chair
- Talking on the phone
- Talking to another person
- Walking past carrying objects
- Lying on the floor
- Sit while covering your eyes, facing dog
- Doorbell/knocking

Sit/Down Stay- Practice stays on or in various objects. Slowly increase the amount of time you ask your dog to hold his position. Stays can be maintained on a pause table, platform, cot, natural object, bench, ottoman or in a hoop, box or kennel. Be sure you are not placing them in an uncomfortable position.

Waiting at Door- Ask your dog to wait while you go through the door. While they remain on the opposite side of the threshold, wait for him to look at you before releasing him through the door. Slowly increase duration of eye contact before releasing. Reward with a treat and verbal reinforcement while he is waiting and giving eye contact.

Wait Line- Make two lines 4'-6' apart. Have dog wait behind first line, while you move to the second line. Face your dog and release to come to you. If he breaks before you release him, return him to the first line and try again. To make more difficult, place a long line on your dog, increase the distance between lines to 8'-10', working up to 20' or more.

<u>Wall Climb-</u> A competitive sport using a 15' vertical wall marked every 6" and a detachable toy on a pully. Dogs compete at how high they can climb the wall to recover their toy. *GRC Dogsports* offers three levels of classes that incorporate increasingly difficult commands. Good spotting skills are necessary to prevent excessive impact on your dog.

<u>Weight Pulling-</u> You can teach your dog to pull a sled or cart for competition, exercise and fun. *GRC Dogsports* offers a pulling competition incorporating a weighted sled.

<u>Working Walks-</u> To get more from your walks, incorporate a variety of commands. Sit, down, stays, place, coming and heeling with turns are all easily added into a walk, encourage engagement and providing mental stimulation. Urban agility can easily be incorporated into your walks by using the environment as your obstacle course.

The bottom line, challenging your dog mentally will tire him out faster than physical play. Physical play is good for their health and mental games are very good for their mind. Encouraging your dog to learn new things is fun and good for your dog.

Games are both physically and mentally tiring and great for building your relationship with your dog. Training your dog may seem like a lot of work, but if approached as a game with a positive attitude and frequent reinforcement, it is all fun and games to your dog. Constructive games teach your dog to work with you as a team and should be enjoyable for both of you.

Keep in mind, dogs don't know what you want or how to respond to commands naturally. You must teach the response you want and reward the behavior, so they want to repeat it. Dogs don't intentionally defy you; they do what has worked for them in the past or react as their instincts dictate. Do not get angry if they don't respond as you would like. Evaluate your training program looking at how you can break tasks down into smaller steps. This will help you communicate more clearly with your dog.

Part 5- Puppy Selection and Early Development

We frequently assist people during the selection process of finding a puppy or rescue dog for a specific purpose. We commonly seek dogs who can perform service dog tasks, Search and Rescue duties, various performance sports, therapy work, emotional support, companionship or multi-functional purposes.

This section will give insight into the factors we consider when choosing a dog for a specific purpose. If you who already have a dog, there is likely to be another in your future and much of the information is beneficial at all ages.

Choosing a Breed

Dogs are genetically designed to perform a variety of functions. When choosing a breed, it is important to consider the job the dog was bred to do and how that will affect his behavior in the home.

Dogs bred to herd are inclined to nip and control fast moving targets or block your path with their body. Dogs bred to fight other dogs are likely to be aggressive towards other dogs. Dogs bred to run and pull are likely to run and pull. Dogs bred to guard are likely to be territorial. Dogs bred to alert by barking are likely to bark. Dogs bred to hunt are likely to have high prey drive and run off chasing small animals. Dogs bred to retrieve will likely be naturals at retrieving. The list goes on, but all these traits will impact the needs of your dog. You can't get a Border Collie because you think he's cute and think you can train him to be a couch potato. If you want a couch potato, get a Greyhound.

Finding a dog with a suitable personality and capabilities for your lifestyle should be the highest priority, followed closely by soundness and health. It is important to consider the amount of physical exercise, mental stimulation, grooming, food and vet care a particular breed of dog needs.

There are varieties within breeds. Some breeders breed for show, others for work, companionship or just to make money. You will find a huge variance in temperament across these different lines.

Dogs bred to work generally have higher energy and drive, requiring more physical and mental exercise.

Dogs bred for confirmation often have a stockier build, heavier coats and lower drive than working lines.

Dogs bred to be calm companions may not have the energy to keep up with an active family.

Dogs bred for money by backyard breeders and puppy mills are likely to have more health and behavior issues due to genetics, poor care, inbreeding and lack of focus on early development.

Even within a litter of puppies, there will be a variety of temperaments. This is one reason we perform temperament testing. We prefer to perform the Puppy Aptitude Test on the 49th day because this is the best age to get the most accurate insight into their genetic tendencies.

Researching a breed before you commit is recommended. Even if adopting, consider the genetic tendencies of the prominent breed of your rescue.

When researching breeds consider the following:

- What activities do you want to pursue with your dog?
- Are there young children in the household?
- What is the breed bred to do?
- How might the genetic behaviors of a breed impact your household?
- Who is the author of the information you are reading?
- Who are your resources and what bias might they have?
- What is your activity level?
- How much time are you committed to exercising and training your dog?
- What genetic diseases are common within the breed?
- What tests are available to identify genetic diseases?
- What is the average longevity?
- What size dog is best for your activity level, accommodations and needs?

PART 5- PUPPY SELECTION AND EARLY DEVELOPMENT

- What coat type do you prefer?
  - Short, medium or long length, shedding or non-shedding, wiry or fluffy, single or double coat, curly or straight?
- How much grooming are you committed to?
- Do you like facial hair?
- Tail or no tail?
- Prick ear, drop ear or flop ear?
- What color do you prefer?

Double Trouble- Thoughts on Getting Littermates

We recently adopted two Dutch Shepherd puppies to raise and train as Diabetic Alert Dogs. The responsibility of these two project pups is shared between four trainers. They live with us in our homes to learn all the skills and behaviors needed to become service dogs.

The puppies came to us unexpectedly and due to previously scheduled trips and vacations, there were a few days I had these 12-week puppies together. At this point I had Caper for about two-weeks, we were developing a routine and things were getting easier.

These few days with both Caper and Brennan was a great reminder of why we don't recommend getting litter mates or two young puppies at the same time.

We have witnessed many situations where one puppy needed to be rehomed once they matured, due to fighting. I could see that potential in Caper and Brennan given too much time together. They are a very bad influence on each other's behavior and get overstimulated during play frequently.

Even though they are at work with us frequently, we limit their play time and don't allow them to play inappropriately. We want interacting with us to be their priority and do not want them developing undesirable behaviors. When they were given freedom together, in just a few days, I noticed the following changes in their behavior.

They amped each other up if they heard sounds, would get each other barking and jump on anything in the way or charge at fences to find the cause. Their co-reliance on each other created extra courage.

They amplified each other's prey drive. With one, I could redirect verbally; with two, they both blew me off. Together they pestered the cats relentlessly; individually it was easily managed.

They became very pushy, vying for attention and possessions. They were very competitive with each other; play would become rough and turn into squabbles. They became overstimulated frequently.

I could see how co-dependencies develop and the affect it had on training. They were both less engaged with me, were more worried about each other than listening to me, were less patient with obedience training and less likely to offer behaviors. They were so competitive for the treats that they wouldn't remain calm enough to hold a position. They would disengage from me and distract each other.

Individually, the puppies would play for a while and nap a lot. Together they took shorter and fewer self-induced breaks. They would lie down for a bit, then one would get the other going. I would see them make eye contact from across the room and off they would go again. They just kept each other going long after they were tired, causing them to become overtired and very irritable.

Both puppies are easy to manage, motivated to work and well-behaved individually. It would take a lot of diligence and purposeful training for these two pups to meet their potential in a home together. They have a much higher chance of success separately. Caper and Brennan are not a unique case, these extra challenges come with getting litter mates. Sometimes it works out, sometimes it doesn't.

If you find yourself in the position of having littermates or multiple young dogs the following are some must haves. Many of these tips apply to single puppies as well.

> Crate training puppies and teaching them to be comfortable in a crate by themselves will be extremely helpful in managing the puppies, house training, giving breaks, and individual time.

> Breaks are as important as exercise and training. Mandatory nap times help the puppies retain what they've learned, is important for development and gives you a break as well.

> Frequent, short, individual training sessions are necessary to give the puppy the best learning environment. It is hard to teach a

puppy if they are distracted by their sibling. Train behavior individually and once they each understand, work them together.

Individual training is important for building your relationship with each puppy. If the puppies get all their entertainment from each other, it will be difficult to get them to respond to you. They can also become co-dependent and very stressed if separated. Creating independence from each other should be worked on immediately upon bringing them home.

Using house leads on the puppies while loose is very helpful for management. We do not want to have to reach and grab a puppy each time he is misbehaving to move or redirect. Grabbing them can cause avoidance or nipping. It is best to have a short, light lead on that you can reach for to manage the puppy.

Playtime together should be managed so they don't become over stimulated and frequent breaks should be implemented. Put them away before they become overtired and irritable. Be sure to give them a lot of individual play time as well. Playing is a great way to build your value in the eyes of your puppy.

When working the puppies together, start by having one handler per puppy. This will help provide a more structured, consistent lesson.

Teaching the puppies to wait at doors and gates should begin immediately. They become very competitive about getting out the door first and create chaos. Take control of doors right away. This is a safety issue and will help set you up for more controlled walks in your future.

Manding is the act of the puppy offering a sit to ask for things. A good breeder will have started this with the litter. If not, you can start this right away by waiting for the puppy to sit or at least have four on the floor before you give any attention or treats. They may not understand at first, but once they understand sitting earns them what they want, they will offer it voluntarily. We want manding to become their default behavior.

Puppy proof your house by enclosing an area with the strategic use of X-pens, baby gates, crates and furniture. Make it an area where the puppy is always visible and with easy access to a door near the potty area. Block access to shelves with shoes, books, etc. Be sure they can't chew any cables or wires. Clear or remove coffee and end tables. Check what they have access to when you recline your chair.

The bottom line is, taking on litter mates adds extra challenges to puppy raising. It is important to make individual time for each puppy and give them frequent breaks apart from each other to develop independence. Put one or both away before they become overstimulated to maintain a peaceful environment. Create a set up that your puppies can be successful in both as individuals and pack members.

Breeder Selection

My goal is to find a physically healthy and emotionally stable pup, who shows the potential of meeting my or my client's goals.

I developed a Breeder Questionnaire to help me gather and record information while researching breeders.

Breeders should be educated about their breed and incorporate appropriate health tests. I look for good or better hips and elbows, clear eyes, clear genetic screenings and tests specific to common issues within each breed. I want to see the breeder is taking advantage of available tests and utilizing the information to arrange the best pairings.

The temperament of the puppy is extremely important. The best insight we have into their potential is to look at their ancestors. Fear and aggression are highly heritable traits. I would avoid purchasing a puppy from lines who exhibit these traits. Additionally, I want to perform a Puppy Aptitude Test as close to 7 weeks as possible.

The importance of early training and hereditary traits are commonly overlooked and undervalued. Breeders should provide an enriched environment, early training and socialization. They should be easy to work with, allow visiting and involvement in the decision making.

A good breeder will be vested in your success and work with you on proper placement. They will be interested in your goals, your environment, the care you provide and have contracts addressing health guarantees, return policies, spay/neuter policies, etc.

Use the information obtained in the questionnaire to assist you in finding that diamond-in-the-rough breeder who can give you and your pup the most optimal start in reaching your goals. If you need help, we are happy to provide this service at *A Canine Experience, Inc.*

Breeder Profile Questionnaire

Breeding Kennel Name: **Breed of Dog:**
Breeder Name: **Phone #:**
Location: **E-mail:**

Breeding Program Objectives?
Breeders goal/objective:
Temperament of lines:
      Working/show:
Service work, sport, pet, SAR, hunting, herding, etc:

What is the environment like in which the puppies are raised?
How many dogs are on the premise/size of breeding facility:
How often are puppies available:
      Litters per year on average:
How are the puppies housed?
How are the puppies fed?
What type of interaction/socialization do puppies get?
Environmental exposure/enrichment:
Individual handling away from litter:
Following any programs like *Puppy Culture*:
Family lifestyle (kids, active/quiet):
What is the set up for eliminating?
      At what age?
Exposure to crate:
Age of Placement:

Application/Contracts
Application process:
Deposits:
Spay/neuter requirement:
Placement requirements:
Return policy:
Health guarantee:
Ongoing support:
Vaccination/worming program:

Process of choosing homes?
Allow us to temperament test:
Pick of litter/choice position:
Visits during development:

Available to meet and provide facility tour?
Interested in working with us on DAD or other projects:
Early scent imprinting:
Communication, availability and follow through:
Overall gut feeling:

Litter Details
Due date, 49th Day, placement date:
COI:

About Dam - Available to meet?

Name:
Age:

Number of litters:
Average size:
Diet and nurturing during pregnancy:
Attentive to pups:
Desirable traits:
General temperament:
      Aggression:
      Fear:
      Drive:
Physical traits:
Structure and movement:
Weaknesses:
Titles/certifications:
OFA/PennHIP score:
Elbow score:
OFA CAER registry number:
Breed specific genetic disease test results:
Pedigree registry:

CHIC certification:
Ancestry- health and performance:
Offspring- health, performance and traits:
Breeding arrangements:

About Sire- Available to meet?

Name:
Age:

Number of offspring:
Desirable traits:
General temperament:
     Aggression:
     Fear:
     Drive:
Physical traits:
Weaknesses:
Structure and movement:
Titles/certifications:
OFA/ PennHIP score:
Elbow score:
OFA CAER registry number:
Breed specific genetic disease test results:
Pedigree registry:
CHIC certification:
Ancestry- health and performance:
Offspring- health, performance and traits:
Breeding arrangements:

Health and Genetic Testing

Radiographs and genetic testing are an important part of a quality breeding program. It is standard for quality breeders to have eyes tested annually, hip and elbows x-rayed at two years of age and to test breeding stock for known breed specific genetic diseases. OFA is a database that records health information and uses the information for research, to help breeders make better pairing decisions and gives buyers access to test results.

Orthopedic Foundation for Animals (OFA)- Chic Program

The OFA created the Canine Health Information Center (CHIC) by partnering with participating parent clubs to research and maintain information on the health issues prevalent in specific breeds. They've established a recommended protocol for breed-specific health screenings. Dogs tested in accordance with that protocol are recognized with a CHIC number and certification.

A dog achieves CHIC Certification if it has been screened for every disease recommended by the parent club for that breed *and* those results are publicly available in the database.

The CHIC program provides accurate information about the results of a breeder's health testing. For diseases that are limited to phenotypic evaluations, there are no guarantees. However, the probability that an animal will develop an inherited disease is reduced when its ancestry has tested normal. Further, as more DNA tests become available and the results are entered, the OFA database will be able to establish whether progeny will be clear, carriers, or affected. (OFA CHIC)

To see tests recommended by breed go to: https://www.ofa.org/browse-by-breed.

The chart on the next page shows other databases that are useful for researching breeds, pedigrees and health certifications.

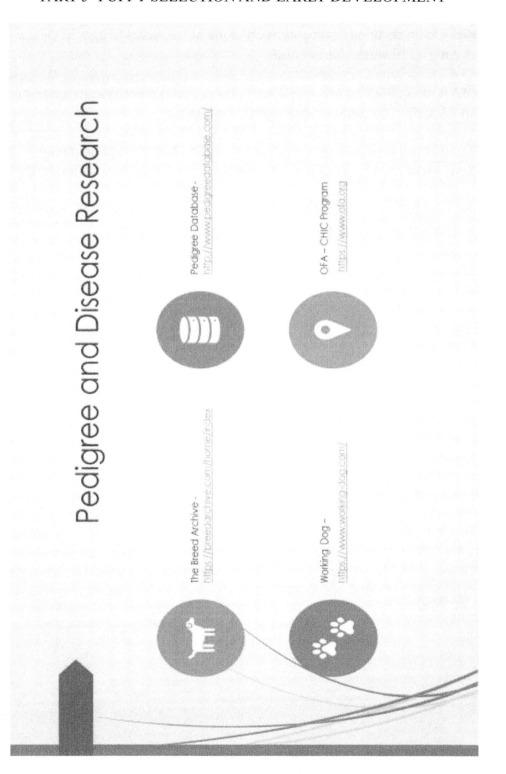

Hips- To be certified, radiographs are done at two years of age for OFA or as early as 16 weeks for PennHIP.

OFA is recognized by AKC and is scored on a seven-point system based on an evaluation by three independent radiologists.

PennHIP is based on a Quantitative Calculation Index 0-1 (0 being the best) performed by a trained veterinarian. (Based on a measurement.)

You may see scores on pedigrees from tests performed in other countries with different scoring systems. See the comparison chart below.

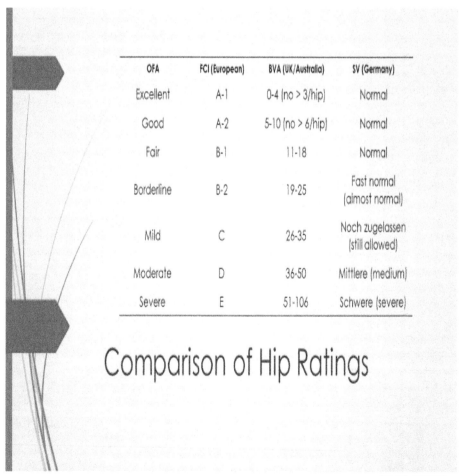

OFA	FCI (European)	BVA (UK/Australia)	SV (Germany)
Excellent	A-1	0-4 (no > 3/hip)	Normal
Good	A-2	5-10 (no > 6/hip)	Normal
Fair	B-1	11-18	Normal
Borderline	B-2	19-25	Fast normal (almost normal)
Mild	C	26-35	Noch zugelassen (still allowed)
Moderate	D	36-50	Mittlere (medium)
Severe	E	51-106	Schwere (severe)

Comparison of Hip Ratings

(OFA HIPS)

Elbows- To be certified radiographs are done at two years of age with five grades from Grade 0 Normal to Grade III Severe. See chart below to see OFA and UK scoring.

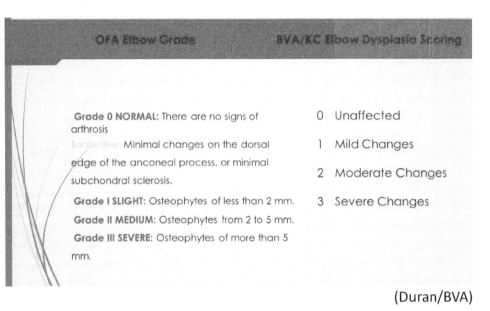

OFA Elbow Grade	BVA/KC Elbow Dysplasia Scoring	
Grade 0 NORMAL: There are no signs of arthrosis	0	Unaffected
Borderline: Minimal changes on the dorsal edge of the anconeal process, or minimal subchondral sclerosis.	1	Mild Changes
	2	Moderate Changes
Grade I SLIGHT: Osteophytes of less than 2 mm.	3	Severe Changes
Grade II MEDIUM: Osteophytes from 2 to 5 mm.		
Grade III SEVERE: Osteophytes of more than 5 mm.		

(Duran/BVA)

Eyes- Should be tested annually by an AVCO certified ophthalmologist annually and recorded in the CAER registry.

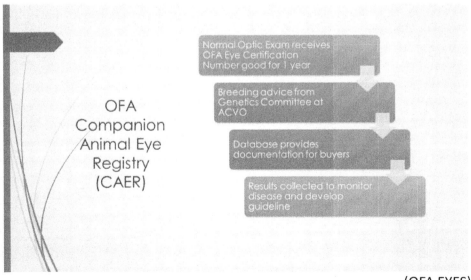

OFA Companion Animal Eye Registry (CAER)

- Normal Optic Exam receives OFA Eye Certification Number good for 1 year
- Breeding advice from Genetics Committee at ACVO
- Database provides documentation for buyers
- Results collected to monitor disease and develop guideline

(OFA EYES)

Genetic Testing and Screening- Tests are a definitive diagnosis of a specific disease. Screening is less costly and will help determine if a diagnostic test is needed. Below is a chart with popular companies who perform DNA screening and testing.

Health and Genetic Tests

Paw Print Genetics Diagnostic Tests	Paw Print Genetics Canine Health Check	Embark	Wisdom Panel
Definitive diagnosis of specific disease	Screen 150 Diseases	Screen 170+ Diseases	Screen 140+ diseases
Tests each mutation 2x with independent methods	Tests each gene region 1X	Breed determination back to Great Grandparents; Relative Finder with updates	Breed determination back to Great Grandparents
Breed specific for disease, coat, color and traits	No coat or trait testing	Breed ID over 250 breeds; 20+ trait tests	250+ breeds, types and varieties; Traits and predicted weight
Access to geneticist or vet for questions	Access to geneticist or vet for questions	Access to geneticist or vet for questions, ongoing research	Access to geneticist or vet for questions

Testing for Genetic Disorders: DNA samples are collected by cheek swab or blood draw.

Paw Print Genetics- Go to https://www.pawprintgenetics.com/ to enter a breed of dog to see a recommendation of breed specific tests. PPG provides swab kit and return envelope, are located in Spokane, and return results within 14 days.

- PPG is a diagnostics test where the results are a definitive diagnosis of the specific disease being tested.
- PPG tests each disease mutation twice, with two independent methods. This standard is something found in human grade genetic laboratories where accuracy of the genetic testing is highly regulated.
- The testing at PPG is breed specific for disease, coat color and traits.
- When ordering testing with PPG you are able to voluntarily post results on their sister website Paw Print Pedigrees. Paw Print Pedigrees allows you to showcase your breeder program and the genetic health of the dogs that you have tested with PPG.
- Good resource for researching breeders at www.pawprintpedigrees.com.
- Access to a geneticist or vet and be able to talk about any questions you might have before ordering, while waiting for your test results and/or after you receive your results.

Canine Health Checks by *Paw Print Genetics-* Screens for about 224 diseases. Diagnostic tests are available for an additional fee. CHC provides swab kit and prepaid return envelope are located in Spokane and return results in 14 days.

- CHC is a screen, where the result gives you an estimate of the level of risk and would help you determine if a diagnostic test is justified.
- CHC tests each disease region once, which is comparable to most other animal genetic laboratories.

- CHC screens for 224 diseases regardless of breed and up 31 trait testing.
- The CHC results can be shared through social media with friends and family.
- Gives access to a geneticist or vet to talk about any questions you might have before ordering, while waiting for your test results and/or after you receive your results.

Wisdom Panel- Provides screening for 150+ diseases plus breed detection and traits. They provide swab kit and prepaid return envelope and return results in 2-3 weeks.

- Covers 250+ breeds, types and varieties.
- Results for 140+ disease-causing genetic mutations including disease descriptions and indication of level of severity.
- Breed determination back to the great-grandparent level in both family tree and percentage formats.
- Information about the traits your dog may exhibit.
- A predicted weight profile.

Orthopedic Foundation for Animals (OFA)- Is a very large, highly recognized databank of DNA and disease statistics. An excellent resource with breed specific testing recommendations compiled from intensive research.

- DNA testing includes automatic registration into the OFA databank.
- Approved labs, specialists or own analysis.
- Supports public access to information.
- Good resource for researching breeders.

Environment and Upbringing

The environment and atmosphere the puppies are raised in will have a huge impact on their development. The effect begins during the mother's pregnancy. The health and emotional state of the dam will influence the learning of the puppies.

From the very beginning there are age appropriate interaction to stimulate growth and development. For example, a Biosensor Program to stimulate the neurological system from three-16 days will have a positive change for life by increasing their tolerance to stress.

Socialization, environmental exposure, housetraining, manding, recovery from stress, problem solving, and basic obedience can and should be started well before being placed in permanent homes.

Optimally, all breeders would only breed dogs who have sound conformation, are healthy and exhibit stable temperament. Additionally, they'd follow a puppy raising program that maximizes early development.

The best breeders follow a program such as *Puppy Culture* to develop the puppies socially, emotionally and physically at a young, impactful age.

The first 12 weeks of a puppy's life are an underestimated, critical time period that is often overlooked by prospective owners and breeders. We coach and assist people who do not know what to look for in finding the right puppy and breeder. We've also come realize many people don't understand the power of early development and training, thus the reason for the following section. Below are highlights from the *Puppy Culture* DVD series which focuses on the developmental period from prenatal until 12 weeks of age.

Early Development in Puppies

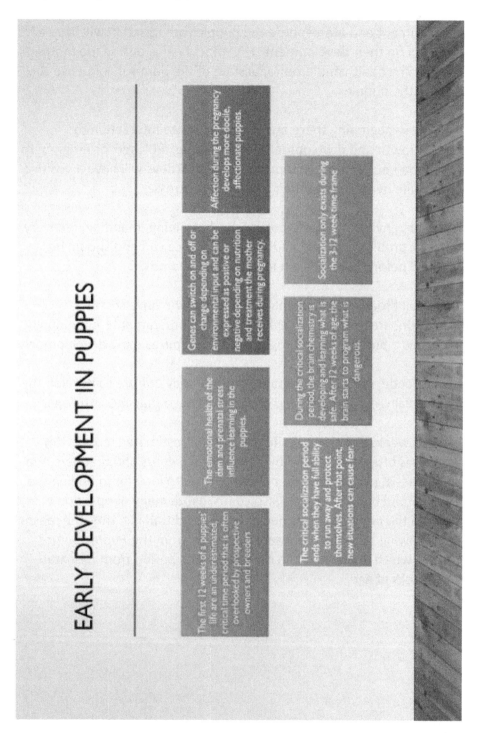

PART 5- PUPPY SELECTION AND EARLY DEVELOPMENT

Puppy Culture the Powerful First 12 Weeks That Can Shape Your Puppies Future **DVD Series Highlights©**

(See full summary in the Appendix)

The *Puppy Culture* proposition states that the first twelve weeks of life can change the puppy's outcome by what is taught. It takes more time and effort to create change in an older dog, but training is still effective.

Prenatal Period

The emotional health of the dam and prenatal stress influence learning in the puppies. Affection during the pregnancy develops more docile, affectionate puppies.

Neonatal Period 0-14 Days

Dogs are born before being fully developed. From 0-14 days, they can't hear, eliminate on their own, regulate body temperature or walk.

Stimulating the neurological system during the three-16 day window will have a positive change for life by increasing tolerance to stress, increasing resistance to disease, strengthening the immune system, strengthening the heart and developing a faster adrenal system.

Transitional Period 14-21 Days

Puppies transform from being deaf, blind and helpless to having the ability to see, hear, toddle and play. Generally, day 16-17, they begin eliminating, walking and will try to move away from the elimination area. Teeth start forming along with an interest in food and lapping fluids.

Critical Socialization Period Three-12 Weeks

During this period, it is easy to form attitude and behavior forever. The opportunity is lost once it is over. Socialization only exists during the three-12-week time frame

A solid socialization program includes seven key components to nurture development:

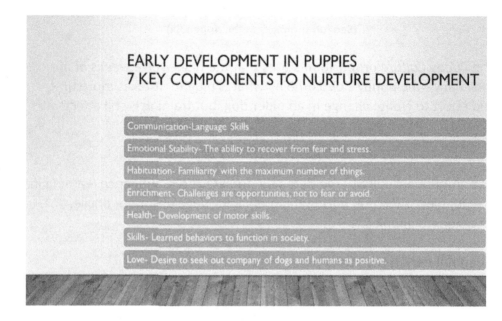

EARLY DEVELOPMENT IN PUPPIES
7 KEY COMPONENTS TO NURTURE DEVELOPMENT

- Communication-Language Skills
- Emotional Stability- The ability to recover from fear and stress.
- Habituation- Familiarity with the maximum number of things.
- Enrichment- Challenges are opportunities, not to fear or avoid.
- Health- Development of motor skills.
- Skills- Learned behaviors to function in society.
- Love- Desire to seek out company of dogs and humans as positive.

Three Weeks- Social Creatures Emerge

Puppies begin to solicit and accept invitations to play, defend themselves from being hurt, ask for attention and show emotional responses when receiving attention.

It is important to set up an environment that avoids conflict.

At three and a half weeks introduce a litter box, grass pellets work well.

Teach recovery from fear by conditioning to be emotionally resilient from three-four weeks.

Four Week- Dreadnoughts

Physical exercise is a key component in enrichment and helps the brain grow.

Teaching communication earlier gives better cognitive advantage.

At four weeks, introduce the communication trinity:

1. Training an indication marker (clicker)
2. Offered behaviors
3. Manding

Puppies learn most rapidly using short sessions with breaks in between. For puppies under five months, one-three minutes training sessions with 15-minute breaks are optimal.

Response fatigue has developed when there are less rights and more wrongs.
Optimally, the session would end prior to fatigue developing.

Five Weeks- Fear and Fun

Sudden spikes in fear are common at about five weeks and again, even stronger, at eight weeks. This normally levels off around 10 weeks.

You want to take care not to induce fear. Provide small amounts of new exposure that allow for a quick recovery. Enriching experiences and exposure are important without a negative experience.

Provide a safe environment with places to retreat and hide. Do not force or coax the puppy.

Six Weeks Party Animals

At six weeks, the part of brain that governs reasoning is unformed, but has almost adult capacity to take in information and form emotional reactions.

During this curiosity period, they have the lowest fear compared to their high level of curiosity. This is the best time to introduce them to a lot of different people objects and surfaces.

Little Monsters- Behavior problems avoided are problems that don't have to be fixed. Most behavior problems are created in first 12 weeks of life.

Three categories of behavior problems:
1. Loose Screw- happens but is rare.
2. Not a problem, rather an expression of inheritable trait found to be inconvenient.
3. Missed pieces of education.

Seven Weeks- Every Puppy Has a Story

This is the optimal age for Temperament Testing.

Eight-Nine Weeks- Ready or Not

Puppies are entering a strong fear imprint period, an unusually sensitive age, typically seen in the eighth to ninth week. Use caution, this is not the time to introduce new experiences, a negative experience can affect the puppy the rest of his life.

Showing signs of fear to normal objects or sounds are the most recognizable signals they are in a fear phase.

It is a huge red flag if a breeder places puppies under seven weeks of age. Better breeders keep the puppies until they are older.

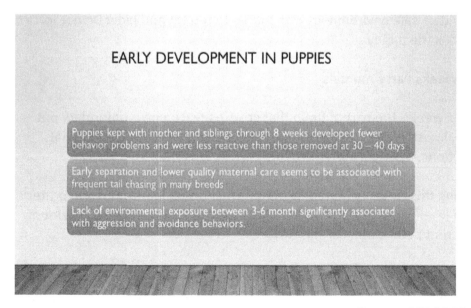

EARLY DEVELOPMENT IN PUPPIES

Puppies kept with mother and siblings through 8 weeks developed fewer behavior problems and were less reactive than those removed at 30 – 40 days

Early separation and lower quality maternal care seems to be associated with frequent tail chasing in many breeds

Lack of environmental exposure between 3-6 month significantly associated with aggression and avoidance behaviors.

PART 5- PUPPY SELECTION AND EARLY DEVELOPMENT

Under 12 Weeks- Social Graces

Start training simple foundational behaviors. There are many benefits of early formal training including:

> Puppies are more likely to benefit from experience rich socialization experiences.

> Puppies taught with rewards before 12 weeks of age will develop a training relationship that will imprint.

> As an adult, they will understand training is good and seek out opportunities to work with you.

> Early training is easy and it only takes one-two sessions to teach the basics.

Gazes and Bonding- Choices in Rearing and Training

Research shows exchanging gazes raises pituitary oxytocin levels, the love hormone that binds us together. In the study, oxytocin levels only rose when the dog chose to look at the person.

Running with the Big Dogs- Socialization for Puppies 10-12 Weeks Old

Continue challenging puppies during training sessions. Fifteen minutes of mental exercise will tire them out versus hours of physical exercise.

Dogs don't generalize well. Have them meet people of various ages, gender, ethnicity, looks, wearing different things, etc. Expose to people carrying various objects, pushing/pulling items, creating different movements, engaging in a variety of activity and so on.

Balancing Risks and Benefits of Early Socialization

With some precautionary measures, the risk is minuscule that a puppy will come down with disease versus the high risk of behavior problems without proper socialization. (Killion et.al.)

Temperament Testing

Optimally, Puppy Temperament Testing is performed on the 49th day because their brains are neurologically complete, but minimally affected by experience and learning. At seven weeks of age, puppies have learned inherited behaviors without many experiences, so you can see the raw material of their temperament. They have not yet learned undesirable behaviors so the personality can be evaluated objectively. Testing before or after the 49th day, affects the accuracy of the test.

We use the Volhard Puppy Aptitude Test (PAT) for the initial evaluation of the puppies. The PAT is comprised of 10 tests scored from 1-6. The complete test description and explanation of results is included in the appendix under "Choosing Your Puppy (PAT) -Volhard Puppy Aptitude Testing."

Once we have completed the PAT, we perform additional exercises with our top picks. The additional exercises will be determined based on the goals for the puppy. These may include following in a new environment with challenges, coming games, hotdog trails or scent imprinting, navigating obstacles, reaction to a bird, playing with additional toys, unfamiliar surfaces, visual stimuli, reaction to a leash, etc. When possible, we will come back another day to introduce additional challenges.

We will also discuss the PAT results with the breeder to see if they are in-line with what the breeder has been seeing. The test is a moment in time and several factors can impact the results. The most common interference is due to tired puppies. It can be difficult to time the test for when they are prime, since they like to play, sleep, eat and repeat.

The test components and summary of scoring are shown in the charts below.

Ten Attributes Tested

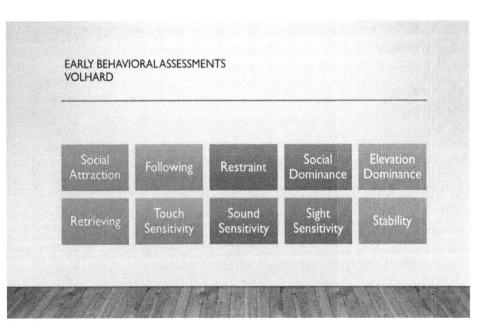

Understanding PAT Scores

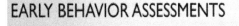

EARLY BEHAVIOR ASSESSMENTS

Volhard Assessment is a standard test optimally performed on the 49th day.

Ten exercises applied in new environment by stranger, scored 1-6

1's Desire to be Pack Leader, Predisposition to aggression, Experienced home, no children or elderly

2's Difficult to manage, Self-Confident, needs strict rules, lots of exercise, experienced home, no kids or elderly

*3's High energy, Regular Exercise, Good with people/dogs, learns quickly, 2nd time owner

*4's Easy to train, quiet, good with kids/elderly, good 1st time owner, needs regular exercise

5's Fearful, shy, needs care in handling, run away from stress, sensitive to sound, new people and environments, need quiet home, tendency to bite if cornered

6's Independent, unlikely to bond, doesn't need people

PART 5- PUPPY SELECTION AND EARLY DEVELOPMENT

Puppy aptitude testing gives great insight into a puppy's natural tendencies, but its value has limitations. Test results are best considered in combination with other factors and information gathered in the research process.

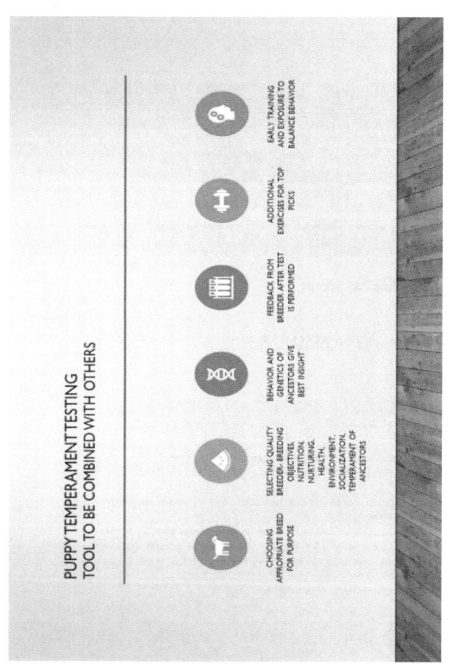

Part 6- APPENDIX

Using Scent Pans to Teach Your Dog to Find an Object

Scent Pans: A typical scent pan has a small hole in the top, we made some of ours out of plastic dog dishes and drilled holes in the bottom - flip it upside down and it's ready to go!

When training, master each step before progressing to the next level. **You always want to end successful. Always reward your dog**. If your dog has a favorite toy, you can use that as a reward instead of treats.

- Place three pans on the floor and let your dog watch while you put the treat under the pan. Most dogs will be naturally curious and go over and start sniffing the pans. Watch for any change in interest, say "Good" and lift the pan to reward with the treat.

- Repeat this a few times, rewarding quickly for showing interest, then end the game and pick up the training aids.

- If your dog doesn't show any interest in the pans, have your dog follow your hand with the treat to the bowl. Encourage him to smell the hole in the pan you've placed the treat under by tapping on it. Once your dog stiffs the pan with the treat, quickly lift the pan up and let him have the treat.

   TIP: If your dog is struggling, turn the pans up right and place treats in them. Allow your dog to explore, realize there are treats in the pan and let him eat them. Once he is comfortably taking treats from the pan, flip it back over and put the treat under it. When your dog is finding the treats without your help, move back to the previous step.

- Once your dog has the idea to sniff the hole in the pan with the treat, fake which pan you're putting the treat under. I use the term "Find It" to start the game and "Check Here" to have him check a pan. Reinforce with "Good Check" each time they sniff a bowl. Have your dog sniff each pan until he finds the one with the treat. Quickly remove the pan telling him "Good Find" and let him have the treat. Once you've mastered this step move on to the next step.

- Don't let your dog see you put the treat under the pan. It's best if you have someone who can help you by walking your dog away while you hide the treat and then bring him back to you when you're done. Your helper can also hide the treat for you.

- After your dog is able to identify which pan has the treat, encourage him to signal by pawing the pan, sitting beside the pan or lying down. You can give him a command asking for the desired behavior. For example, if you want your dog to indicate they found the item by lying down, tell him "Down" when he shows interest in the correct pan. When he downs, lift the pan while saying "Good Find" and let him take the treat. From now on, ask for the designated indicator to earn the reward. Choose only one indicator and stick with it. Once he consistently searches all three pans and indicates, move to the next step.

- If he can search three pans, he can search multiple pans. Start adding more pans to the game. Spread out the pans into a long line and have him search the line. Continue incorporating the indicator before giving him the reward.

- Add the item you want him to find under the pan with the treat. If you want to teach him to find your keys, put the keys and the treat under the pan and continue practicing. Do this a few times, it won't make much difference to your dog, because the treat is still there. When rewarding, have your dog sniff the object and reward repeatedly before placing back under a pan for another round.

- Hide only the item you want to teach your dog to find under a pan. He may need a little help at this point, because up to now he's had the food smell to motivate him. Lower your expectation and reward for any change in behavior as you did in the beginning. You may have to tap the pan to get him to smell it, then immediately reward him over the hole in the pan. Pick up the pan, let him check out the object and reward repeatedly for sniffing it.

- Once he understands searching for the object, add the indicator back in by cuing the behavior and rewarding immediately upon success.

- Start making the game more difficult by adding pans, moving them into a circle instead of a line, start pushing them further apart and putting them in areas like the corner, under a chair, behind a piece of furniture, etc.

- Start placing the pans on surfaces with varying levels, on the chair, in an open cupboard, on a shelf, on a short table. This teaches them to search above the level of the floor. Once he is finding the item consistently at multiple levels and indicating move to the next step.

- Take the pans away and hide the item with a treat in a fairly simple place. This is a confusing step for your dog, because the pans, which have been a visible aid that you're working, are gone. He again may need a little assistance. Use your command "Find It" to let him know you're working and the command "Check Here" to get him looking in different places. Only use the treat with the item a few times to get him to understand the change in the game. Lower your criteria and reward for any change of behavior or interest.

- Hide the item only in a fairly simple place, reward him with a treat for finding. Again, lower your criteria and reward for any change of behavior or interest.

- Once he understands the searching for the object without aids or treats, reincorporate the indicator by cuing the behavior. Reward immediately once the behavior is achieved. Continue cuing the behavior until he becomes reliable and responds quickly.

- Once he responds quickly to the cue for the alert, start waiting a few seconds to see if he will offer the behavior. Reward immediately when he indicates with the trained alert behavior. If he doesn't indicate, work with cuing a bit more, giving opportunities to alert without cuing by withholding the cue for a few seconds intermittently.

- Once your dog's alerting reliably, work on his commitment to the scent by building duration between the alert and the reward. Encourage him to stay with the odor in the alert position. Build the commitment slowly, do not ask for too much too quickly. We want to build commitment, not frustration.

- Slowly increase the difficulty of the hiding spot placing the item only and rewarding him with treats.

- Have someone else hide the item without you knowing where it is. This is the true challenge to determine if your dog really understands the game.

- **Always reward your dog for his work!**

A few notes about search games and scent training:

The search should always be successful, meaning there is always something to find and it gets found. Always pick up the training aids at the end of the session, so they don't sniff without reward and loose interest.

If you are continuously needing to give extra help to succeed, back up a step or two. When increasing difficulty lower your criteria for indicating until they are confident with the change.

It is good to have multiples of the object you are teaching your dog to find. This way, if you actually lose the object, you can plant one in case your dog can't find the one you're looking for. Working without success is very discouraging to them and they will lose faith that there is something to be found. You must keep in mind the level of their training.

Be careful not to tell your dog where the item is with your body language. In a couple steps I have you helping them, but once they get it, be conscientious of your body language. Let your dog stop you. Don't look at the item or change your pace as you approach. You must act consistently during the exercise. If you want them to look in a certain area tell them to "Check Here" but stand back and let them look. Make sure to have them check places that the item is not hidden in as well to ensure that the command doesn't become a give-away.

If your dog is toy motivated and you would like to use a toy as a reward, replace the treats with the toy. When the item is found, use the toy to play with your dog as the reward. This will only work with very toy driven dogs. Common toys used are balls and tugs.

The alert behavior needs to be trained separately and fluent when you begin cuing it at the find.

Variations can be made to these steps and still be successful. For example, you could train all the steps with treats or toys and switch to another object later, or you could focus on all the search components and add the trained indicator later.

There are many ways to imprint your dog on the smell of an object. One simple way is to let your dog sniff an object, mark with "Good" and reward repeatedly. Another is to place the object in a low distraction area, allow your dog to explore, mark and reward any change in behavior or interest. The object could be placed in a box, under a pan, in a suitcase or something that will attract your dog to it.

Only focus on one new variable at a time.

Make it fun. This is a positively reinforced game. Do not correct your dog, even if they are wrong. Ignore the behaviors you don't want and reward the ones you do. He doesn't get reinforced for wrong choices, so there will be no reason for him to continue offering them. Have big parties with new successes and when overcoming challenges

Choosing Your Puppy- Wendy Volhard's Puppy Aptitude Test©

Choosing the Right Puppy for the Right Home!

Getting a dog or puppy on impulse is rarely a good idea. Remember that dogs, like cars, were designed for a particular function. You need to decide what you want, a Corvette or a Suburban, a Fox Terrier or a Newfoundland.

When the various breeds were originally developed, there was a greater emphasis on the ability to do a job, such as herding, guarding, hunting, drafting, etc., than appearance. If a particular breed interests you, find out first what the dog was bred to do. There are so many different breeds to choose from and if there is a secret to getting that "perfect puppy," it lies in doing your homework.

Deciding What Kind of Dog to Get

The well-trained dog begins with some idea of what role the dog is expected to play in your life and then selecting a dog that is suitable for the job. Following are some of the reasons for selecting a dog:

- Companionship
- Playmate for the kids
- Protection
- A special activity, such as hunting, herding, breeding, showing in conformation, or competing in performance events
- Status symbol (not wise)
- A combination of the above

Some dogs are able to fill all of these expectations, while others have more limited talents.

Getting a dog for a status symbol usually means one of the guarding or rare breeds, and often these represent some special challenges. If you want a rare breed, first find out why it is such a rare breed and if there are any potential drawbacks.

Conversely, one of the most popular dogs and number one in American Kennel Club registrations is the Labrador Retriever. The reason is simple – a Lab is a good multipurpose dog that can serve as a companion and playmate for the kids, is naturally protective, generally good health, makes a good guide dog, and with little time and effort can be transformed into a well-trained dog.

You also need to take into account your own lifestyle and circumstances. For most of us this means a dog that can satisfy our need for companionship, is easily trained and doesn't require a lot of upkeep.

Keeping up Appearances

Everyone has his or her own preference and there is an enormous choice, from the four-pound Yorkshire Terrier to the 200-pound Mastiff. Many dogs come in different sizes, such as Poodles, or Schnauzers. Other have a smaller version that is similar in appearance, such as Collies and Shelties, or Dobermans and Miniature Pinschers, or German Shepherds and Corgis, or Greyhounds and Whippets, the "poor man's race horse".

Tidbits: Poodles and Terriers don't shed but have to be groomed regularly. Unless you are willing to spend the time and effort learning how to do it yourself, this means periodic visits to a professional groomer, an expensive proposition.

Breeds with long hair require more upkeep than those with short hair. Pretty obvious when you think about it, but often completely overlooked when selecting a puppy or dog. Some breeds, like Briards, Poodles, Wirehaired Dachshunds and Terriers don't shed, a most desirable feature. On the other hand, unless you are willing to learn how to groom your dog, it means regular visits to the grooming parlor, visits that are not cheap.

Some breeds, such as terriers and some of the herding dogs, bark a lot more than others. If you live in an apartment, such a dog would not be a good choice.

Bet You Didn't Know: Why does the breed standard for many dogs sound so similar when describing the dog's temperament? Because so many of them were written by the same man. In 1874, J.H. Walsh, under the pen name of Stonehenge, published "The Dog: Its Varieties and Management in Health," the first major effort to describe the more than 60 breeds recognized at that time.

The Time Factor

In selecting a dog or puppy be aware of the time factor. How much exercise does this particular breed require and are you in a position to give it to your dog? Some breeds require less exercise than others, but many require two daily 20-minute walks, at a minimum, and some, such as the Sporting breeds, much more. Just letting the dog out in a backyard is not sufficient.

In the selection process you need to remind yourself continuously that your dog is going to be with you anywhere from eight to 16 years. And, the older he gets, the more important regular exercise becomes.

How much time do you have available to devote to training that cute little bundle of fur? If you have little or no more that 10 to 15 minutes a day, then you need to select a breed that is easily trained and doesn't require much exercise.

What are You Looking For?

A good place to start is *The Complete Dog Book* by the American Kennel Club, which describes the breed standards for the different breeds recognized by that organization. Two other excellent resources are *Roger Caras Dog Book: A Complete Guide to Every AKC Breed* (Dorset Press, 1992) and *Paws to Consider: Choosing the Right Dog for You and Your Family* by Brian Kilcommons and Sarah Wilson (Grand Central Publishing, 1999).

Another wealth of information can be found at dog shows, where you can see a large variety of breeds and talk to their owners and breeders. But remember, they are obviously and naturally biased.

PART 6- APPENDIX

To help you get the dog you want we have devised a simple test that is amazingly accurate in predicting inherited behavioral tendencies and how the puppy will turn out as an adult.

What is Puppy Testing?

Some of the tests we use were developed as long ago as the l930's for dogs bred to become Guide Dogs. Then in the 1950's, studies on puppies were conducted to determine how quickly they learned. These studies were actually done to identify children's learning stages.

Top Dog Tips: The ideal age to test a puppy is at 49 days of age when the puppy is neurologically complete and it has the brain of an adult dog. With each passing day after the 49th day the responses will be tainted by prior learning.

Later on in the early 60's more tests were developed to determine if pups could be tested for dominance and submission. These tests determined that it was indeed possible to predict future behavioral traits of adult dogs by evaluating puppies at 49 days of age. Testing before or after that age, effected the accuracy of the results, depending on the amount of time before or after the 49th day.

We took these tests, added some of our own, and put together what is now known as the Volhard Puppy Aptitude Test, or PAT. PAT uses a scoring system from 1-6 and consists of ten tests. The tests are done consecutively and in the order listed. Each test is scored separately and interpreted on its own merits. The scores are not averaged, and there are no winners or losers. The entire purpose is to select the right puppy for the right home.

The Tests Consist of the Following:

1. Social Attraction - degree of social attraction to people, confidence or
    dependence.
2. Following - willingness to follow a person.

3. Restraint - degree of dominant or submissive tendency and ease of handling in difficult situations.
4. Social Dominance - degree of acceptance of social dominance by a person.
5. Elevation - degree of accepting dominance while in a position of no control, such as at the veterinarian or groomer.
6. Retrieving - degree of willingness to do something for you. Together with Social Attraction and Following a key indicator for ease or difficulty in training.
7. Touch Sensitivity - degree of sensitivity to touch and a key indicator to the type of training equipment required.
8. Sound Sensitivity - degree of sensitivity to sound, such as loud noises or thunderstorms.
9. Sight Sensitivity - degree of response to a moving object, such as chasing bicycles, children or squirrels.
10. Stability - degree of startle response to a strange object.

During the testing make a note of the heart rate of the pup, which is an indication of how it deals with stress, as well as its energy level. Puppies come with high, medium or low energy levels. You have to decide for yourself which suits your lifestyle. Dogs with high energy levels need a great deal of exercise and will get into mischief if this energy is not channeled into the right direction.

Finally, look at the overall structure of the puppy. You see what you get at 49 days age. If the pup has strong and straight front and back legs, with all four feet pointing in the same direction, it will grow up that way, provided you give it the proper diet and environment in which to grow. If you notice something out of the ordinary at this age, it will stay with puppy for the rest of his life. He will not grow out of it.

How to Test

Here are the ground rules for performing the test:

- The testing is done in a location unfamiliar to the puppies. This does not mean they have to be taken away from home. A 10-foot square area is perfectly adequate, such as a room in the house where the puppies have not been.

- The puppies are tested one at a time.
- There are no other dogs or people, except the scorer and the tester, in the testing area.
- The puppies do not know the tester.
- The scorer is a disinterested third party and not the person interested in selling you a puppy.
- The scorer is unobtrusive and in position to observe the puppy's responses without having to move.
- The puppies are tested before they are fed.
- The puppies are tested when they are at their liveliest.
- Do not try to test a puppy that is not feeling well.
- Puppies should not be tested the day of or the day after being vaccinated.
- Only the first response counts!

Top Dog Tips: During the test, watch the puppy's tail. It will make a difference in the scoring whether the tail is up or down. The tests are simple to perform and anyone with some common sense can do them. You can, however, elicit the help of someone who has tested puppies before and knows what they are doing.

1. Social attraction - the owner or caretaker of the puppy places him in the test area about four feet from the tester and then leaves the test area. The tester kneels down and coaxes the puppy to come to him or her by encouragingly and gently clapping hands and calling. The tester must coax the puppy in the opposite direction from where it entered the test area.

Hint: Lean backward, sitting on your heels instead of leaning forward toward the puppy. Keep your hands close to your body encouraging the puppy to come to you instead of trying to reach for the puppy.

2. Following - the tester stands up and slowly walks away encouraging the puppy to follow. Hint: Make sure the puppy sees you walk away and get the puppy to focus on you by lightly clapping your hands and

using verbal encouragement to get the puppy to follow you. Do not lean over the puppy.

3. Restraint - the tester crouches down and gently rolls the puppy on its back and holds it on its back for 30 seconds. Hint: Hold the puppy down without applying too much pressure. The object is not to keep it on its back but to test his response to being placed in that position.

4. Social Dominance - let the puppy stand up or sit and gently stroke it from the head to the back while you crouch beside it. See if he will lick your face, an indication of a forgiving nature. Continue stroking until you see a behavior you can score.

Hint: When you crouch next to the puppy avoid leaning or hovering over the puppy. Have the puppy at your side with both of you facing in the same direction.

Top Dog Tips: During testing maintain a positive, upbeat and friendly attitude toward the puppies. Try to get each puppy to interact with you to bring out the best in him. Make the test a pleasant experience for the puppy.

5. Elevation Dominance - the tester cradles the puppy with both hands, supporting the puppy under its chest and gently lifts it two feet off the ground and holds it there for 30 seconds.

6. Retrieving - the tester crouches beside the puppy and attracts its attention with a crumpled-up piece of paper. When the puppy shows some interest, the tester throws the paper no more than four feet in front of the puppy encouraging it to retrieve the paper.

7. Touch Sensitivity - the tester locates the webbing of one the puppy's front paws and presses it lightly between his index finger and thumb. The tester gradually increases pressure while counting to ten and stops when the puppy pulls away or shows signs of discomfort.

8. Sound Sensitivity - the puppy is placed in the center of the testing area and an assistant stationed at the perimeter makes a sharp noise, such as banging a metal spoon on the bottom of a metal pan.

9. Sight Sensitivity - the puppy is placed in the center of the testing area. The tester ties a string around a bath towel and jerks it across the floor, two feet away from the puppy.

10. Stability - an umbrella is opened about five feet from the puppy and gently placed on the ground.

Scoring the Results

Following are the responses you will see and the score assigned to each particular response. You will see some variations and will have to make a judgment on what score to give them.

SOCIAL ATTRACTION
    Came readily, tail up, jumped, bit at hands 1
    Came readily, tail up, pawed, licked at hands 2
    Came readily, tail up 3
    Came readily, tail down 4
    Came hesitantly, tail down 5
    Did not come at all 6

FOLLOWING
    Followed readily, tail up, got underfoot, bit at feet 1
    Followed readily, tail up, got underfoot 2
    Followed readily, tail up 3
    Followed readily, tail down 4
    Followed hesitantly, tail down 5
    Did not follow or went away 6

RESTRAINT
    Struggled fiercely, flailed, bit 1
    Struggled fiercely, flailed 2
    Settled, struggled, settled with some eye contact 3
    Struggled, then settled 4

No struggle 5
No struggle, strained to avoid eye contact 6
SOCIAL DOMINENCE
Jumped, pawed, bit, growled 1
Jumped, pawed 2
Cuddled up to tester and tried to lick face 3
Squirmed, licked at hands 4
Rolled over, licked at hands 5
Went away and stayed away 6
ELEVATION DOMINANCE
Struggled fiercely, tried to bite 1
Struggled fiercely 2
Struggled, settled, struggled, settled 3
No struggle, relaxed 4
No struggle, body still 5
No struggle, body froze 6

RETRIEVING
Chased object, picked it up and ran away 1
Chased object, stood over it and did not return 2
Chased object, picked it up and returned with it to tester 3
Chased object and returned without it to tester 4
Started to chase object, lost interest 5
Does not chase object 6

TOUCH SENSITIVITY
8-10 count before response 1
6-8 count before response 2
5-6 count before response 3
3-5 count before response 4
2-3 count before response 5
1-2 count before response 6

SOUND SENSITIVITY
Listened, located sound and ran toward it barking 1
Listened, located sound and walked slowly toward it 2
Listened, located sound and showed curiosity 3
Listened and located sound 4

Cringed, backed off and hid behind tester 5
Ignored sound and showed no curiosity 6

SIGHT SENSITIVITY
Looked, attacked and bit object 1
Looked and put feet on object and put mouth on it 2
Looked with curiosity and attempted to investigate, tail up 3
Looked with curiosity, tail down 4
Ran away or hid behind tester 5
Hid behind tester 6

STABILITY
Looked and ran to the umbrella, mouthing or biting it 1
Looked and walked to the umbrella, smelling it cautiously 2
Looked and went to investigate 3
Sat and looked, but did not move toward the umbrella 4
Showed little or no interest 5
Ran away from the umbrella 6

What do the Scores Mean?

The scores are interpreted as follows:

Mostly 1's –
- Strong desire to be pack leader and is not shy about bucking for a promotion.
- Has a predisposition to be aggressive to people and other dogs and will bite.
- Should only be placed into a very experienced home where the dog will be trained and worked on a regular basis.
- *Top Dog Tips: Stay away from the puppy with a lot of 1's or 2's. It has lots of leadership aspirations and may be difficult to manage. This puppy needs an experienced home. Not good with children.*

Mostly 2's –
- Also has leadership aspirations.
- May be hard to manage and has the capacity to bite.
- Has lots of self-confidence.
- Should not be placed into an inexperienced home.

- Too unruly to be good with children and elderly people, or other animals.
- Needs strict schedule, loads of exercise and lots of training.
- Has the potential to be a great show dog with someone who understands dog behavior.

Mostly 3's –
- Can be a high-energy dog and may need lots of exercise.
- Good with people and other animals.
- Can be a bit of a handful to live with.
- Needs training, does very well at it and learns quickly.
- Great dog for second time owner.

Mostly 4's –
- The kind of dog that makes the perfect pet.
- Best choice for the first-time owner.
- Rarely will buck for a promotion in the family.
- Easy to train, and rather quiet.
- Good with elderly people, children, although may need protection from the children.
- Choose this pup, take it to obedience classes, and you'll be the star, without having to do too much work!
- *Tidbits: The puppy with mostly 3's and 4's can be quite a handful but should be good with children and does well with training. Energy needs to be dispersed with plenty of exercise.*

Mostly 5's –
- Fearful, shy and needs special handling.
- Will run away at the slightest stress in his life.
- Strange people, strange places, different floor or ground surfaces may upset him.
- Often afraid of loud noises and terrified of thunderstorms.
- When you greet him upon your return, may submissively urinate.
- Needs a very special home where the environment doesn't change too much and where there are no children.
- If cornered and cannot get away, he has a tendency to bite.

Mostly 6's –
- So independent that he doesn't need you or other people.
- Doesn't care if he is trained or not - he is his own person.
- Not likely to bond to you, since he doesn't need you.
- A great guard dog for gas stations!
- Do not take this puppy and think you can change him into a lovable bundle - you can't, so leave well enough alone.
- *Top Dog Tips: Avoid the puppy with several 6's. It is so independent it doesn't need you or anyone. He is his own person and unlikely to bond to you.*

Interpreting the Scores

Few puppies will test with all 2's or all 3's - there will be a mixture of scores.

For that first time, wonderfully easy to train, potential star, look for a puppy that scores with mostly 3's and 4's. Don't worry about the score on Touch Sensitivity - you can compensate for that with the right training equipment.

Tidbits: It's hard not to become emotional when picking a puppy - they are all so cute, soft and cuddly. Remind yourself that this dog is going to be with you for eight to 16 years. Don't hesitate to step back a little to contemplate your decision. Sleep on it and review it in the light of day.

Avoid the puppy with a score of 1 on the Restraint and Elevation tests. This puppy will be too much for the first-time owner.

It's a lot more fun to have a good dog, one that is easy to train, one you can live with and one you can be proud of, than one that is a constant struggle.

Choosing a Breeder

Once you have done your research and you have decided which breed is most suited to your lifestyle and expectations, it is time to choose a breeder. You can meet breeders at dog shows, through the local newspaper, or popular dog magazines, such as *The American Kennel Club Gazette*, *Dog World* or *Dog Fancy*.

Here are some of the criteria you want to follow in selecting a breeder:

- Choose an experienced breeder, one who has had several litters and who knows his breed.
- Choose a breeder who has shown his dogs and has done some winning, which is a fairly good indication that his or her dogs conform to the standard of the breed and will grow up looking like the dogs you saw that attracted you to the breed in the first place.
- Choose a breeder who is using our Puppy Aptitude Test. If he or she hasn't heard of it, show it to them; avoid one that says, "I don't believe in that."
- Choose a breeder whose dogs are certified by the applicable registries against breed-related genetic disorders, such as eyes, hips, etc.
- Choose a breeder where you can interact with adult dogs and get some idea how long they live.
- Choose a breeder where the dogs are well housed and everything is clean.

The majority of breeders today show a great willingness to have their puppies tested and are interested in the results. It shows them the inherited behaviors of their breeding stock, valuable information for future breeding. The results make it easier for them to place the right puppy into the right home where people will be happy with them. After all, no breeder wants a puppy returned when it's eight months old and may have been ruined by being improperly brought up.

Whatever you do, don't try to pick a puppy by having the entire litter together - you will not be able to pick the right one for you. Always interact with a puppy individually, away from his litter mates.

Getting a Dog from a Shelter

Don't overlook an animal shelter as a source for a good dog. Not all dogs wind up in a shelter because they are bad. After that cute puppy stage, when the dog grows up, it may become too much for its owner. Or, there has been a change in the owner's circumstances forcing him or her into having to give up the dog.

Most of the time these dogs are housetrained and already have some training. If the dog has been properly socialized to people, it will be able to adapt to a new environment. Bonding may take a little longer, but once accomplished the result is a devoted companion.

While you can't use the entire puppy test, there are some tests that will give you a good indication of what to look for.

1. Restraint - try putting the dog into a down position with some food, and then gently rolling him over and see what happens. If the dog jumps up and runs away or tries to bite you, this is not the dog for you. Rather look for a dog that turns over readily, but squirms around a bit. Apply just enough pressure to keep the dog on its back; ease up if it struggles too much. Intermittent squirming is OK, constant squirming is not OK.

2. Social Dominance - directly after the Restraint Test, if the dog didn't struggle too much and if you think it's safe, try sitting the dog and just stroking him, getting your face relatively close to him talking to him softly, to see if he licks you and forgives you for the upside down experience. A dog that wants to get away from you is not a good candidate.

3. Retrieving - crumple up a small piece of paper and show it to the dog. Have him on your left side with your arm around him and throw the paper with your right hand about six feet, encouraging the dog to get it and bring it back. You are looking for a dog that brings the paper back to you.

Guide dog trainers have the greatest faith in this test. A dog that retrieves nearly always works out to be a Guide Dog because it indicates a willingness to work for the owner. Other organizations that use dogs from a shelter, such as those who use dogs to sniff out contraband or drugs, and police departments, place almost sole reliance on this test. They know that if a dog brings back the object, they can train him to do almost anything. Wherever you get your dog, use the tests that you can do and act accordingly. By the way, it's not too late to use some of the tests with the dog you already have. It just might explain some of your dog's behaviors.

The Least You Need to Know

- There are many breeds to choose from and if there is a secret in getting that "perfect puppy," it is doing your homework.
- A good place to start is, *The Complete Dog Book* by the American Kennel Club, which describes in detail the different breeds recognized by that registry.
- Carefully consider the time you have available for the necessary up-keep and exercise the dog requires.
- Don't get a dog on impulse!
- Use the Volhard Puppy Aptitude Test in selecting your dog, whether a puppy or an older dog.

Jane Killion's Puppy Culture- The Powerful First 12 Weeks That Can Shape Your Puppies Future©

Summary taken from the DVD set, focusing on the developmental period from prenatal until 12 weeks of age.

The *Puppy Culture* Proposition states that the first twelve weeks of life can change the puppy's outcome by what is taught. It takes more time and effort to create change in an older dog, but training is still effective.

Prenatal Period

The emotional health of the dam and prenatal stress can influence learning in the puppies. Genes can switch on and off or change depending on environmental input, and can be expressed as positive or negative depending on nutrition and treatment the mother receives during pregnancy. Affection during the pregnancy develops more docile, affectionate puppies.

Gestation lasts about 63 days. X-rays are helpful in knowing the number of pups to expect and help determine when and how to intervene.

Neonatal Period 0-14 Days

Dogs are altricial species, meaning the young are born before being fully developed. The eyes and ears are closed to protect them from light and sound that would otherwise be damaging. They are born helpless and fully dependent on their parents; in turn they have a more flexible imprint period than precocial species like foals and goslings who need to imprint quickly for survival.

When pups are born, they have no ability to wander and are completely protected by their parents, so fear doesn't develop until later. They are unable to flee, so fear is a useless response. The social significance is that they have a longer, more accommodating time frame for social attachments, which remains somewhat flexible over their lifetime. The process is socialization and forms a basis for our ability to bond with dogs.

The critical socialization period ends when they have full ability to run away and protect themselves. After that point, new situations can cause fear.

From 0-14 days, they can't hear, eliminate on their own, regulate body temperature or walk. They communicate by nuzzling and pull themselves towards the warmth using heat sensors.

In the first 24 hours, colostrum is produced providing maternal antibodies that wear off after a few weeks. The pups can only absorb antibodies in the first 18 hours of life. After 18 hours, the intestinal wall closes, so antibodies pass through rather than being absorbed.

Puppies' brains send out impulses to build muscles, visible by twitching and pulsing while they sleep. Appropriate stress and struggles help with development. Research shows slight stress has long term positive effect while the neurological system is developing.

Dr. Bottaglia, with *Breeding Better Dogs,* recommends the Biosensor Program as protocol to stimulate neurological system. Stimulating the neurological system during the three-16-day window will have a positive change for life by increasing tolerance to stress, increasing resistance to disease, strengthening the immune system, strengthening the heart and developing a faster adrenal system.

Biosensor Program:

1) Tactile Stimulation- Use a Q-tip to tickle between toes three-five seconds. Stimulates skin to wake up neurological system.

2) Hold the head up and tail down for five seconds. This causes the blood to drain from brain, stimulating the heart to pump blood to brain.

3) Hold the head down for five seconds. Too much blood to the brain causes the neurological system work in a different way.

4) Supine Position- Hold on back for five seconds. Struggling stimulates the neurological system to go to work.

5) Thermal Stimulation- Place a wet washcloth in the refrigerator for 30 minutes. Place the puppy on the cold cloth for five seconds. This stimulates the neurological system to respond to temperature change.

Why do this? Because it is unlike other handling and it stimulates the neurological system.

How often? One time per day from three days to 16 days old to reap benefit.

More is not better! It's too much if the puppy is already stressed or if you're doing longer than times above.

Transitional Period 14-21 Day

Puppies transform from being deaf, blind and helpless to able to see, hear, toddle and play. The average age can vary for each puppy, one must observe to know what period they're in. Generally, day 16-17, they begin eliminating, walking and will try to move away from the elimination area.

The transitional period begins when the eyes open and ends when they startle by hearing a sound. Barking, growling, tail wagging and body responses develop. Teeth start forming with an interest in food and lapping fluids. By day 21, the breeder should supplement the diet with meat and goat's milk.

PART 6- APPENDIX

Critical Socialization Period Three-12 Weeks

During this period, it is easy to form attitude and behavior forever. The opportunity is lost once it is over. It takes a minimal amount of time and effort to create change compared to an older dog, who will take more time and effort to achieve a limited change.

Biology Lesson for the Day: During the critical socialization period, the brain chemistry is developing and learning what is safe. After 12 weeks of age, the brain starts to program what is dangerous. They can then become afraid of the unknown.

Socialization only exists during the three-12-week time frame. Beyond 12 weeks, it is no longer socializing. You can train by counter conditioning, desensitizing and teaching things are safe, but these are harder processes and don't always work because they use different brain chemistry.

Learning to be a dog through socialization consists of more than exposure. Exposure is only one component of the process by which the puppy gains skills to live in society and develop emotional bonds. Dogs must learn two concurrent processes: Dog society and human society.

Emotional intelligence is the ability to connect on a deep, trusted level and can be taught during the socialization process.

A solid socialization program includes seven key components to nurture development:
- Communication-Language Skills.
- Emotional Stability- The ability to recover from fear and stress.
- Habituation- Familiarity with the maximum number of things.
- Enrichment- Challenges are opportunities, not to fear or avoid.
- Health- Development of motor skills.
- Skills- Learned behaviors to function in society.
- Love- Desire to seek out company of dogs and humans as positive.

Three Weeks- Social Creatures Emerge

Puppy's begin to solicit and accept invitations to play, defend themselves from being hurt, ask for attention and show emotional responses when receiving attention.

It is important to set up an environment that avoids conflict. The dam should be able to retreat to avoid puppies when weaning. Growling and snapping is not natural or in the best interest of the pups. In a study of 600 pups, those raised with moms who snapped and growled to wean are less outgoing and less likely to approach strangers. Moms who used avoidance and non-confrontational methods produce puppies who were more social, more playful, less fearful and more likely to approach strangers. Always provide the mom a way to retreat by using high places and barriers.

Pups at this age do lots of growling as they learn to use ritualized threats to avoid violence. This is a normal developmental phase; they are learning a set of signals to resolve disputes without violence.

Keep the puppies' nails trimmed short to make it comfortable for mom to be with the pups. It is painful to nurse when the nails are long. Trimming nails desensitizes the puppies' feet to being handled, helps give proper conformation while they are learning to walk, helps to keep legs and feet in the correct position to grow properly and is easiest to do while they are sleeping.

Introduce a new toy or object to the whelping box each day. New toys, exercises and challenges enrich the environment. Animals raised in stimulus rich environment with exercise produce larger brains, up to 5% more brain mass. The cells that form from exercise, enrichment and stimulation effect the area of the brain that impacts learning, memory and emotional responses.

PART 6- APPENDIX

Puppies raised in an enriched environment form 25-200% more neuro connections resulting in better retention, more stability, better recovery, improved learning, less fearfulness and better ability to cope with stress.

The Enrichment Effect: Develop social attraction to people by inviting as many people over as possible. Use precautions by removing shoes and washing hands. Have guests change their clothes if they've been around other dogs. The benefits outweigh risks.

At three and a half weeks introduce a litter box- grass pellets work well. Not only does this provide a potty area for the puppies giving a jump start on house training, but walking on this new surface also provides motor coordination and stimulation.

Teach recovery from fear by conditioning to be emotionally resilient from three-four weeks. Startle with sounds, movements, sensations etc. The more times they are surprised and recover from being startled at this age, the more developed the no fear response. We are triggering the startle recovery cycle and exercising the recovery muscle. At three weeks they have a startle response but recover quickly. Studies show they have no fear response, thus providing a short period of time to exercise the recovery muscle without psychological damage.

Begin taking puppies out individually to promote human bonding and help prevent separation anxiety.

Four Weeks- Dreadnoughts

Physical exercise is a key component in enrichment and helps the brain grow. An area to run freely assists with development and lessens contention in the litter. Provide a large area with a potty spot, toys, things to climb on and explore. Change the daily routine with new people, dogs, objects and sounds. Add learning and problem-solving activities to develop more stable, less stressed, less frightened pups with better memory and capability for learning.

Set up appropriate level of challenges, like barrier challenges keeping in mind they can't see well yet. Teaching them to deal with frustrations now, reduces aggressive frustration in the future.

The Communication Trinity- Three Core Concept

Teaching communication earlier gives better cognitive advantage.
At four weeks, introduce the communication trinity:

1) Training to indication marker (Clicker)- Classically conditioned reinforcement creates involuntary physiological response. Click=Food

2) Offer Behaviors- Use a short box and click any behavior that involves the box. Operant conditioning teaches them to offer behaviors, to think past getting what they want, helps with impulse control and teaches delayed gratification.

3) Manding- Teaching puppies to ask by sitting, not jumping. The cue of human presence should indicate to sit versus jump. Click when puppy backs off, then work on sit. This is not training to sit or off on command, we are teaching human = sit without using verbal cues.

Pups are preprogrammed to jump, teaching an alternative action gives the puppy a voice. Correcting shuts down their voice. Depriving social animals of voice is psychologically damaging.

Puppies learn most rapidly using short sessions with breaks in between. Distributed learning is likened to a computer where 1's earned rewards and 0's earned no reward. Puppies sort data while they are sleeping.

Reponses earning rewards are permanently remembered and responses without reward get swept away.

Under 12 weeks age, the optimal working/rest ratio is six minutes of training/30 minutes of rest. Two-minute power trainings are effective. Short sessions are more effective and motivational. For puppies under five months, one-three minutes training sessions with 15-minute breaks are optimal. Response fatigue has developed when there are less rights and more wrongs. Optimally, the session would end prior to fatigue developing.

Five Weeks- Fear and Fun

As pup's approach five weeks, they begin developing fear response and caution is required. During fear imprinting periods, one single frightening experience can cause a life-long lasting reaction. Sudden spikes in fear are common at about five weeks and again even stronger at eight weeks. This normally will level off around 10 weeks. These are sensitive fear periods even if signs are non-apparent or short.

You want to take care to not induce fear. Provide small amounts of new exposure that allow for a quick recovery. If introduced to something new and the puppy doesn't quickly recover, take it down a notch. Never present something truly terrifying to a puppy.

Enriching experiences and exposure are important without a negative experience. Provide a safe environment with places to retreat and hide. To feel safe, they must feel in control. Do not force or coax the puppy. Create positive experiences and provide them with training to overcome fear.

Here's a strategy to help a pup overcome fear of a tarp. Start with something smaller, like a plastic bag and work your way up to a tarp. Do not coax, lure or cheer to go over. Shower with praise and affection when they touch on their own. If you cheer while they are afraid, you reinforce the fear. Stay passive and reward any interaction with tarp.

Six Weeks- Party Animals

At six weeks, the part of brain that governs reasoning is unformed, but has almost adult capacity to take in information and form emotional reactions.

They are entering their peak socialization period. During this Curiosity Period, they have the lowest fear compared to their high level of curiosity. This is the best time to introduce them to a lot of different people. Puppy parties should be well planned training and socialization sessions. Take caution because the same social sensitivity, from three-12 weeks, that allows a puppy to accept something with as little as one exposure, also allows them to imprint a fear of a bad experience in as little as one exposure. Error on side of quality over quantity using puppy savvy visitors. Have a dinner party, so the puppies get use to people, laughing, talking loudly, moving about, variety of smells, etc.

Training on specially designed equipment such as a Buja Board (low wobble board), low dog walk and shoot help develop tolerance. Allow the puppies to decide if they want to explore the equipment, never force them. Hold short sessions of no more than two minutes per piece of equipment and a total of six minutes. Take 15-minute breaks with a goal of three sessions.

Chute- Start without the fabric on the chute. Once you can call back and forth through the opening, replace the fabric and hold chute open so he can see out the other side. Gradually hold the chute open less and less until it is fully closed.

Dog Walk- Click and treat each step. Use a spotter to support with their arm. Don't push the puppy past his level of comfort.

PART 6- APPENDIX

Buja- Start on downside and support the board so it won't move. Click and treat for one foot on the board. Once he understands being rewarded for one foot on, hold out for two, then three, then four feet on.

The Straight Poop- Potty Training Fundamentals

Move the puppies to a bigger pen. An 8'X12' pen with a potty area can be made using three overlapping x-pens. You can then unhook the overlap to make a barrier for cleaning. A separate potty area is important because they instinctively want to keep the den clean. It is important for the breeder to keep the litter box and weaning pen clean for health and ease of house training. You want them to be used to keeping their living area clean.

Puppies do not have a lot of control over their bladder and bowels under 12 weeks of age and often don't even realize they need to go. Try to foresee when they will need to go and be prepared with slip on shoes and a jacket near the door. Typically, they'll need to go out about 10 minutes after the start of a play session, 15 minutes after eating, upon waking up, anytime they stop what they're doing and starts walking around or sniffing. They will also need to go out at least once an hour during the day. If they are near the door, take them outside.

When you cannot watch the puppies, put them where they cannot make a mistake. An X-pen attached to a crate for a den with a potty and play area is optimal. Keep the crate door open. Withhold food three hours before bedtime and water one hour before bedtime. Take outside immediately before putting to bed.

Don't close the crate door until he can go five hours without pottying. Set an alarm to let him out at five hours.

If you catch him in the act of pottying in the house, do not scold. He will perceive he is being scolded for going in front of you and find a safer place to go. He will not want to go in front of you outside either. Don't assume he understands or feels ashamed, he is hiding because he is confused by your behavior.

Little Monsters

Behavior problems avoided are problems that don't have to be fixed. Most behavior problems are created in first 12 weeks of life. Three categories of behavior problems:

1- Loose Screw- happens but is rare.
2- Not a problem, rather an expression of inheritable trait found to be inconvenient.
3- Missed pieces of education or conditioning during the critical period resulting in expression of default genetic material. Strong intervention between three and 12 weeks is needed to shape a dog in a way you want to live. Even the best trainers are working to correct symptoms, not causes. One should look at raising dogs without behavior problems.

Biting- Love Hurts

Getting a puppy to not bite is a function of how you interact with the puppy.

Don't play in ways that make him crazy or overstimulated. You can't play wild games and expect him not to bite.

Limit the kind of interactions you play with your puppy. Structure interactions that teach him how to properly play in a calm and gentle way.

Using intermediary toys to prevent him from biting your hands is helpful. Hand games invite biting.

PART 6- APPENDIX

Calmness is a behavior to be practiced and can be trained like any other behavior. The calmer your interactions are, the calmer he will act and the less he will bite.

If he starts biting, pick him up and turn him away from you. Puppies are biting machines. Keep hands safe by holding the puppy with your hands out of the way. Hold him and gently massage until he calms. This technique is less about correcting and more about avoiding.

Movement is a cue to bite. If he bites while walking or running, stop moving. Use food and praise to reinforce walking next to you without biting.

Stop playing and give the puppy a break before he becomes over tired and starts getting mouthy.

Biting kids is not about dominancy. The definition of dominant is in control of resources, children have more access to resources than dogs. Children interact in excited ways and react in a stimulating way when the puppy bites. Work with the kids and puppy to have calm interactions.

Managing Biting- Yelping and rolling the lip can amp the dog up more. You may need to put the puppy away if the biting can't be managed.

Management strategies may include prying off an object, picking up facing away from you, putting away for a break or having a training session marking and rewarding for walking nicely without biting. It is a judgement call if you should work on training or just manage it at the time. You may not be able to play all the games you want.

If you manage the biting for the first month or two, he will grow out of it and it will have a positive impact on your relationship for the life of the puppy.

PART 6- APPENDIX

Everything Here is Mine

It is natural for puppies to guard food. If they didn't in the wild, they would starve. They learn to communicate ownership of resources and avoid conflict by respecting each other's possessions.

According to *Mine! A Practical Guide to Resource Guarding in Dogs* by Jean Donaldson, this is natural behavior and anti-resource protocol should be incorporated into your puppy's early training program.

Why do dogs resource guard? It is a normal, legitimate behavior to guard possessions. Humans don't respect a dog's ownership of resources and believe they should give them up. This is unnatural to dogs and must be taught.

There is a learning moment when a dog first acts possessive. You can snatch it away now, but when they get older and stronger, they may bite. Instead, quickly replace the object with something great, so the puppy begins to feel happy when you take things away. Train with high value, puppy appropriate objects, trade for a high value treat, then give the original object back. Do this over and over so puppy perceives your reaching in as a good thing.

Doing exchanges with all young puppies to avoid resource guarding has high success. This is best done at six-eight weeks. The opportunity is lost by 12 weeks. It is recommended for dog breeders and puppy owners to work anti-resource guarding protocol for all puppies under 12 weeks of age in the following four areas:

Food Dish- Add food to the dish while the puppy is eating. Use something tastier than what is in the dish. We want to develop CER, a Conditioned Emotional Response (happy reaction) when you approach.

Exchange the dish for a treat. Don't hold the treat out as bribe, rather keep it hidden as you approach. Walk up, take the dish away, then offer the treat.

Objects- Exchange an object for a new object. Take the object away, give a payoff, then give the object back. Use a variety of toys and chews. Repeat. Incorporate touching the puppy before the exchange, because some may object to that as well.

Sleeping Locations- Approach the puppy when sleeping in comfy location, give a treat and leave. To prevent lap guarding with small dogs, approach while they are being held and give a treat.

Touchy, Feely Body Handling- People understand hugging and touching as affection, dogs do not naturally understand that. This can be learned. The earlier the start the better.

Breeders should be handling and touching puppies from the time they are born. As they age body handling should be continued, but their social need decreases.

Start rewarding for touch by touching a paw, rewarding, touching an ear, rewarding, etc. Keep the food out of sight of the puppy so as not to frustrate him.

Why not Just Punish?

Positive reinforcement releases dopamine in the brain increasing the bond between dog and owner.

Punishment activates the fear system and can have negative effects. It can illicit an aggressive response in dogs from a simple leash correction or yelling NO.

Small puppies are not physically able to handle physical corrections.

PART 6- APPENDIX

Seven Weeks- Every Puppy is a Story

Testing and Evaluating for placement- Confirmation vs. Temperament

Confirmation: Looking for type closest to breed standard. Qualities best for breeding program.

Temperament: Tested one at time, with an unknown person in new place. Test includes social attraction, desire to follow, reaction to restraint, ability to forgive, reaction to elevation, chase and retrieve, touch sensitivity, sound sensitivity, sight sensitivity, prey drive, startle recovery and reaction to the unexpected. Temperament testing was designed by *Guide Dogs for the Blind*, but there are too many variables to predict success for placement. Testing is useful less as predictive tool and more as diagnostic tool.

Breeders will have a good idea of personalities by this age, but judgement may be clouded by emotion. Nothing replaces a formal evaluation.

Eight-Nine Weeks- Ready or Not?

Puppies are entering a strong fear imprint period, an unusually sensitive age. Typically seen in the eight-ninth week and can last a few minutes or an entire week. A well raised puppy will have good bounce back.

Use caution, this is not the time to introduce new experiences. It is best to shield the puppy during this time. A negative experience can affect the puppy the rest of its life.

It is not good idea to place puppies in homes during this phase. Only introduce them to well balanced, neutral dogs. Resume socialization once the fear period is over.

Showing signs of fear to normal objects or sounds are the most recognizable signals they are in a fear phase.

The best time to rehome is one week after the first set of vaccinations given at nine weeks. Homing at 10 weeks gives the new owner and puppy two weeks during the socialization period to bond and incorporate socialization.

It is a huge red flag if a breeder places puppies under seven weeks of age. Better breeders keep the puppies until they are older.

Puppies need a lot of rest. For one hour of play, they need two-three hours of sleep.

Under 12 Weeks- Social Graces

Recommended reading *When Pigs Fly*, by Jane Killion.

Start training simple foundational behaviors. Recommended skills to begin include recall, walking on leash, sit to ask for things or manding, and crate training.

There are many benefits of early formal training including:

- They are more likely to experience rich socialization experiences.

- Puppies taught with rewards before 12 weeks of age will develop a training relationship that will imprint.

- As an adult, they will understand training is good and seek out opportunities to work with you.

- Early training is easy and your efforts will produce big benefits. They are hungry, socially motivated and it only takes one-two sessions to teach the basics.

Come to Me- Recall

Most breeders use a puppy call such as a high pitched, excitable "puppy, puppy, puppy" when they put food down, a powerfully conditioned reinforcer. Puppies naturally move toward high pitch, fast sounds. Even if the breeder didn't use a puppy call, you can start by incorporating one when putting the food down.

Once the puppy responds excitedly to the puppy call, you can then start adding a recall cue, such as "Come, puppy, puppy, puppy" to pair the signals. The cue will become equally exciting and you can gradually fade out the puppy call.

Caveats- this works because you are creating a classically conditioned, involuntary feeling of excitement. To maintain this feeling, you must give something fantastic when they come to you. Praise may work when they are small, but by 16 weeks of age, food becomes the most preferred form of currency.

Dogs hear in music or tones, so you must always call the same way. Use a tone you would not normally speak in and only means come to you.

Comfort Zone- Crate Training and Preventing Separation Anxiety

Structure and structured rest are more important than freedom. Being lose all the time until they become crazy, cranky, mouthy, tired and misbehaved does no one any good. Pups need a place to decompress, so crate training is essential. Breeders should start this by separating puppies for short times during the critical period. The crate becomes a que to be calm and take a nap. Pups learn to love crate time and are grateful for the break.

Dogs not taught to be alone become upset when isolated and this leads to separation anxiety. They may become destructive and panic.

PART 6- APPENDIX

Separation anxiety takes a lot of time and effort to cure. The desire to not be alone is naturally hardwired into dogs. Their friendly, social nature is why we were able to domesticate them. If not trained otherwise, they will dread being alone.

Crate training is easy to teach at a young age. Ideally, breeders will leave crates with open doors in weaning pen. Even without that, they will take to the crate easily if left available. Leave a crate open in the puppy's public area and they will find it.

If they get use to sleeping in crate with the door open and being away from their siblings, crate training is simple.

To begin crate training, do not feed for few hours prior and remove water one hour prior. Take the puppy out to potty immediately before putting in the crate. Place puppy in the crate with a bone or chew for a few seconds, then open the door and let out before he starts fussing. Do an exchange for the bone. Slowly increase the amount of time the puppy is left in the crate, but don't push it. Return to let out of the crate before they wake up and start fussing.

Pretty Please-Advanced Manding (Automatic Sit)

Puppies should already have learned concept of asking for things by sitting.

Upon approaching the pen, ignore the puppies who are jumping up and give attention/feed the puppies who are sitting. Have every visitor follow the same approach. You may need to start by rewarding the puppies for four on the floor. Be patient and let the puppies figure out the behavior without you telling them.

Once consistently sitting for people, work with a stationary dog and build up to a dog in motion. Get in the habit of waiting for the puppies to sit before you offer food or attention.

Going Places- Leash Walking

Start practicing walking off-leash in safely fenced area, puppies follow anything that moves. Start walking, click and treat anytime they get near your left side. Let the puppy work it out. Once the puppy understands treats come from being by you, start adding two steps, three steps……working up to more steps. Once walking several steps with you, start walking in small circles positioning the puppy on the inside. Once he understands following, change one thing at a time by adding a collar, then a leash. If shaped correctly, the puppy should automatically follow when called and you start walking.

The leash is not a training tool, it is a backup like a climber's safety rope. When the puppy hits the end of the leash, it activates an opposition reflex and they will naturally fight against it. Let the leash out and keep moving forward. Mark and reward when the puppy starts moving back toward you. Avoid tugging on the leash. He will begin to learn to move toward you when feeling the lead tighten. Increase the difficulty by adding more steps a few at a time. Give him a break after a short session, so the puppy has time to process what he's learned.

Short sessions with rest in between is very powerful at a young age. Longer distances and fewer treats will come in time.

You Get What You Pay For

We are often asked when it is the right time to wean the puppy off food in exchange for a behavior. Why be in such a hurry to not give a dog treats? Thin the ratio…sure, but a relationship is a history of reinforcement. The goal should be to find as many opportunities as possible to give a dog a treat. That will build a relationship.

PART 6- APPENDIX

Human entitlement leads people to the idea dogs should just obey because they were given a command. People feel they have been let down if they must pay for a behavior.

The reality is, behavior is a tool animals use to manipulate their environment that consequently help them survive in the world. We can capitalize on this or ignore it at our own peril. It is a myth to think they should just do it.

Gazes and Bonding- Choices in Rearing and Training

Reflect on what you value in a dog. The way dogs look at us creates an indescribable connection. Obedience is important, but it is only a component that should support the human animal bond. Research shows exchanging gazes raises pituitary oxytocin levels, the love hormone that binds us together. In the study, oxytocin levels only rose when the dog chose to look at the person.

Shaping dogs to want to look at us, and feel safe doing so, will increase the bond.

Running with the Big Dogs- Socialization for Puppies 10-12 Weeks Old

Now that they are vaccinated, meeting lots of safe, new dogs in a managed way is important. Dogs use space to control interactions. If they feel pressured or afraid, they will first run away to diffuse the situation. If there is not enough space and they feel cornered, they will turn to aggression to ward off other dogs. A good set-up will have enough space and a way to escape from larger dogs, like a small fence they can squeeze through or low chair.

Give the puppy control over the situation so he can build his confidence and overcome fears. This should be done off leash because with a leash on, he can't retreat and that makes him feel defenseless. This is the reason for leash reactivity. A trusted, friendly, adult dog and someone who can read body language is helpful. Give the puppy a safe place and allow him to work out in his own time.

Walking with dogs helps them bond and diffuses tension. Do not pay attention or encourage a puppy showing concern, that can reinforce fear. Petting another dog can reassure the puppy. Keep sessions short and give frequent breaks.

Continue challenging puppies during training sessions. Fifteen minutes of mental exercise will tire them out versus hours of physical exercise that will wire them out and they will still be running around biting you.

Dogs don't generalize well. Have them meet people of various ages, gender, ethnicity, looks, wearing different things, etc. Expose them to people carrying various objects, pushing/pulling items, creating different movements, engaging in a variety of activity and so on.

Vaccinations versus Socialization- Balancing Risks and Benefits of Early Socialization

A little about how vaccines work- If the dam was immune to disease, the puppies will also become immune from the mother's milk. There is uncertainty as to when maternal antibodies wear off. The antibodies generally wear off between six and 14 weeks, in some cases could be earlier or later.

Vaccinations work by modifying a disease, so the puppies don't get it, but trick the body into thinking they do so it builds antibodies against the disease. The body will remember how to fight the disease if they are exposed to it again.

If the puppy is vaccinated while he has the mother's antibodies, he will not establish immunity because the mother's antibodies will mask the virus before the puppy's immune system can respond. Three vaccinations are needed because we don' know when the mother's antibodies will wear off and stop interfering with the vaccines. Vaccinations are not recommended under eight weeks because puppies' immune systems are not well established at this age and they would be ineffective. The last vaccination in the series should be given at 16 weeks to be fully effective.

With some precautionary measures, the risk is minuscule that a puppy will come down with disease versus the high risk of behavior problems without proper socialization.

Bring diverse people and variety of objects into the home. Take extra precautions in the outdoor world. Vaccinate seven days prior to outside exposure. Consider the risk to benefit ration. Looking at over 1,000 puppies who went to puppy socialization, 0 developed Parvo; but there have been thousands of cases with behavior problem due to lack of early socialization.

A couple safety guidelines include minimally vaccinating against Parvo and Distemper at seven-eight weeks, seven days prior to exposure. Don't expose your puppy to unvaccinated puppies, dog parks, pet stores, rest stops or other high dog traffic areas. There are no guarantees, but the belief is the benefits outweigh the risks.

Puppy Kindergarten-How to Find a Great Puppy Class

Puppy classes give opportunity for exposure to a variety of people and dogs. Classes should be structured, predictable and include play, training and relaxation sessions. Transition periods are important to learn at a young age.

When looking for a good class, audit first. Classes should be instructor directed with someone who helps the puppies have a good experience. Instructors should be interactive, stepping in when needed, and matching up puppies with similar play style. They should be able to provide help with other issues.

Play groups should be separated by size, age and play style. Puppies should be matched up to experience appropriate, reciprocal play. Pups should have places to escape, an environment that shapes confidence, one person for two-three dogs and safe adult trainer dog(s).

Instructors should be interactive, stepping in when needed. They should be able to provide help with other issues.

There shouldn't be any pig piles, squirt bottles, shake cans, scolding, yelling, pushing pups to play, corrective devices to stop behavior, force or fear tactics. Focus should be on shaping and building positive behaviors.

More is not better; puppies need a lot of rest. When pups are tired, they will start getting snappy and more aroused. After classes, allow them to go home and rest.

A good class agenda will include:

- Sessions transitioning between playing, training and relaxing
- A settling period at beginning of class
- Training exercises like sit, down and calling name
- A play session
- Pass the puppy for treats
- More play
- End with settling and body handling

Transition periods are important to learn at a young age and are broken up into play, train, relax.

PART 6- APPENDIX

Guarantees- The Road Ahead

This is just the beginning. You will need to continue getting your pup out and giving him as many enriching experiences as possible through 18 months. They will not fully develop until three years old and will need to continue participating in positive experiences.

Does all this make a difference?

Working within the parameters of genetics, results will always be better with training and socializations even if doesn't turn out how you want.

BIBLIOGRAPHY

Baer, Nancy. Lead or Be Led. Create Space. Self-published for use at *A Canine Experience, Inc.* 2014.

Baer, Nancy and Steve Duno. Leader of the Pack. New York, Harper Collins, 1996. Copyright © 1996 by Nancy Baer and Steve Duno.

Beuchat, Carol PhD. The Institute of Canine Biology. Genetics of Behavior and Performance. Online Course. 2019.

Brownell, David and Mark Marsolais. The Brownell-Marsolais Scale: A Proposal for the Quantitative Evaluation of SAR/Disaster K9 Candidates. Sept 2000. Internet. https://k9-trader.com/wp-content/uploads/2018/04/Brownell-Marsolais-dog_sreening.pdf ©All Rights Reserved – D. Brownell; M. Marsolais; P. Hawn. 1st Revision: Sept. 2000

BVA British Veterinary Association. https://www.bva.co.uk/media/2791/chs-elbow-dysplasia-2019-v2-web-170419.pdf. PDF download available at: https://www.bva.co.uk/canine-health-schemes/elbow-scheme/

Canine Health Checks. https://www.caninehealthcheck.com/ 509-483-5950

Duran, Dr Margarita. http://www.fci.be/medias/SCI-ART-DYS-COU-MDU-en-1744.ppt Power Point found at Federation Cynologique Internationale. Elbow Dysplasia (ED) Margarita Duran. 2012. http://www.fci.be/en/Hip-and-Elbow-Dysplasia-162.html.

Embark. https://embarkvet.com/. 224-236-2275.

BIBLIOGRAPHY

Grimm, David. How Dogs Stole our Hearts.
http://www.sciencemag.org/news/2015/04/how-dogs-stole-our-hearts.
Internet. The research was published in: *Science* 17 Apr 2015: Vol. 348,
Issue 6232, pp. 333-33 DOI: 10.1126/science.1261022

International Dog Parkour Association. Dog Parkour Instructors Course.
Online. https://www.dogparkour.org/home. 2019.

Killion, Jane et.al. Jane Killion's Puppy Culture-The Powerful First 12
Weeks That Can Shape Your Puppies Future DVD. Madcap Productions,
2014. 5 hour 17 minutes. Copyright @ 2014 PuppyCulture.com©.

OFA CHIC. Orthopedic Foundation for Animals. www.ofa.org/about/chic-
program Internet, Questions about Chic Program: chic@offa.org
https://www.ofa.org/ 573-442-0418.

OFA DNA. Orthopedic Foundation for Animals. DNA Tested Diseases.
https://www.ofa.org/diseases/dna-tested-diseases.

OFA EYE. Orthopedic Foundation for Animals. Eye Certification. PDF
https://www.ofa.org/pdf/eye_flyer_web.pdf found at
https://www.ofa.org/diseases/eye-certification.

OFA HIP. Orthopedic Foundation for Animals. Hip Dysplasia.
https://www.ofa.org/diseases/hip-dysplasia/hip-international-ratings-
matrix.

Paw Print Genetics. https://www.pawprintgenetics.com/. 509-483-5950.

Volhard, Wendy. Choosing Your Puppy (PAT).
https://www.volharddognutrition.com/choosing-your-puppy-pat/.
Internet. Wendy Volhard's Puppy Aptitude Testing © 1981, 2000, 2005.

BIBLIOGRAPHY

Volhard, Wendy. A Personality Profile for Your Dog.
https://www.volharddognutrition.com/canine-personality-profile/
Internet. Wendy Volhard's Dog Personality Profile© 1991, 2000, 2005, 2010.

Wisdom Panel. https://www.wisdompanel.com/wisdom-panel-health/. 888-597-3883

Made in the USA
Monee, IL
16 July 2021

73275646R00115